RONALD REAGAN

RONALD REAGAN

THE PICTORIAL BIOGRAPHY

Sarah Gallick

COURAGE
BOOKS

Printed by Sing Cheong Printing Company Ltd. in Hong Kong

10 9 8 7 6 5 4 3 2 1

Digit on the right indicates the number of this printing.

Library of Congress Cataloging-in-Publication Number 99-72465

ISBN 0-7624-0650-X

Ronald Reagan
The Pictorial Biography
was prepared and produced by
Michael Friedman Publishing Group, Inc.
15 West 26th Street
New York, New York 10010

Editor: Celeste Sollod
Art Director: Kevin Ulrich
Design: Robert Beards Design, Inc.
Photography Editor: Jennifer Bove

Color separations by Spectrum Pte. Ltd. (Singapore)

This book may be ordered by mail from the publisher.
But try your bookstore first!

Published by Courage Books, an imprint of
Running Press Book Publishers
125 South Twenty-second Street
Philadelphia, Pennsylvania 19103-4399

Speech on page 70, "A Time for Choosing," reprinted with the permission of the Ronald Reagan Presidential Foundation.

PAGE 1: President, statesman, leader, Ronald Reagan embodies the American Dream. PAGE 2: Through all the ups and downs of his life, Reagan maintained a rarely broken equanimity that saw him through. PAGE 6: Reagan hammers on one of the last remnants of the Berlin Wall during his visit to Germany in September, 1990; helping to bring down the wall was one of his greatest achievements as president.

In this blessed land, there is always a better tomorrow…
Let history say of us, "These were golden years—when the
American Revolution was reborn, when freedom gained new
life, when America reached for her best…. Let us resolve
that we the people will build an American opportunity society
in which all of us—white and black, rich and poor,
young and old— will go forward together arm in arm…

So we go forward today, a nation still mighty in its youth and
powerful in its purpose. With our alliances strengthened,
with our economy leading the world to a new age of economic
expansion, we look forward to a world rich in possibilities.
And all this because we have worked and acted together,
not as members of political parties, but as Americans.

—Ronald Reagan, second inaugural address, January 21, 1985

Contents

Chapter One
A HERO FROM THE HEARTLAND
1911–1937 . . . . *8*

Chapter Two
HOORAY FOR HOLLYWOOD
1937–1941 . . . . *22*

Chapter Three
A CITIZEN POLITICIAN
1941–1964 . . . . *42*

Chapter Four
A RENDEZVOUS WITH DESTINY
1964–1980 . . . . *66*

Chapter Five
THE REAGAN REVOLUTION
1981–1989 . . . . *86*

Chapter Six
THE REAGAN LEGACY
1989– *108*

Bibliography *116*

Index *117*

A Hero from the Heartland

1911–1937

"Life is just one grand, sweet song, so start the music."

—Motto by Ronald Reagan that appeared under his
photograph in the Dixon High School yearbook, *The Dixonian*, 1928

A few days before Ronald Reagan was elected the fortieth president of the United States, a radio interviewer asked him what it was that the American people saw in him. "Would you laugh if I told you that I think, maybe, they see themselves and that I'm one of them?" he asked. "I've never been able to detach myself or think that I, somehow, am apart from them."

He was tall, handsome, and unmistakably American. He was blessed with a warm and resonant broadcaster's voice that was welcomed into the farms and small towns of the prairie long before his face was famous. His life spanned most of the twentieth century, from the eve of World War I to the dawn of space travel, from the introduction of radio to satellite communications. He was an intimate of heads of state, but he never lost the small-town values that formed his character. And he changed the course of history.

He worked his way through college by washing dishes, and he rose to lead the free world. He became the single greatest force in bringing down the Soviet Union. While his critics scoffed, he led the longest sustained economic recovery since World War II. Throughout his life, he was known for his unfailing optimism and self-deprecating humor.

When he entered political life, he was fifty-five years old and his critics dismissed him as a has-been actor. But in Hollywood, Reagan had learned about trade unions, organized crime, communists, and congressional investigations. That education armed him for battles with student radicals, defiant union bosses, jaded congressional leaders, and totalitarian dictators.

He so rarely showed anger that when he did—at a 1980 campaign debate in New Hampshire and in a 1985 confrontation with Soviet President Gorbachev at Reykjavik—the events were startling and memorable. And he made his point.

ABOVE: Reagan as the successful young broadcaster. His charm and good looks, so evident in this early publicity photo, impressed one visiting star enough to recommend him to her agent when she got back to Hollywood. PAGE 8: Ronald "Dutch" Reagan poses at about twelve years old, just before he entered Dixon High School. His family moved eight times before settling in Dixon when Reagan was nine. He was always proud to call Dixon his hometown.

Like any truly great performer, he made it all look remarkably easy. From the very beginning, the truth was that, underneath, his life was often a struggle, and none of his great achievements came easily.

The All-American

Ronald Wilson Reagan was born to Nelle and Jack Reagan on February 6, 1911, during a terrible blizzard in Tampico, Illinois. Home was a five-room apartment above a bank, which was just about the only contact the family had with money. The new baby was a robust ten-pounder, "a fat little Dutchman" as Jack called him, and for the first twenty-five years of his life he was known as "Dutch." He was also welcomed by his brother, John Neil, known as "Moon" and older by a little more than two years.

For the next nine years, the Reagan family moved frequently. Jack was a charming alcoholic who dreamed of owning the finest shoe store south of Chicago. Bad luck and his own weaknesses would always frustrate that dream. He could spin a good yarn, especially about the fine bootery he would own one day, but meanwhile he had trouble keeping a job as a clerk in a shoe store. Between 1911 and 1920, the Reagans lived briefly on the south side of Chicago (where Jack worked for Marshall Field's Department Store), in Galesburg, in Monmouth, and then back in Tampico while Jack chased his dream.

At home, Nelle saw to her sons' spiritual life, instilling in them traditional Christian values. "I was raised to believe that God has a plan for everyone and that seemingly random twists of fate are all part of His plan," Reagan would later recall. "From my mother, I learned the value of prayer."

At night, while Jack read his newspaper at one end of the kitchen table, Nelle often read classic "boy books" such as *The Three Musketeers* aloud to her sons, following each word with a finger while they watched over her shoulder. By the time he was five, young Dutch could read the entire newspaper to his very proud father.

JACK AND NELLE

The parents of the fortieth president of the United States met over the counter at the J.W. Broadhead Dry Goods Store in Fulton, Illinois, where both of them worked.

John Edward Reagan was born in 1883 to Irish immigrants who came to homestead in Illinois. Orphaned at six, he moved among various elderly relatives until he left school at the age of twelve to work in an aunt and uncle's struggling dry goods store. At sixteen he joined his older brother and sister in Fulton, where they found him a job selling shoes at Broadhead's. He was darkly handsome, a good dancer, and a gifted storyteller, but already a bit too fond of the drop.

Still, he made a powerful impression on Nelle Clyde Wilson, the youngest of six children, who had left her family's struggling farm in northwestern Illinois to work as a shopgirl. They married on November 8, 1904.

Nelle knew she had married a restless man who was burning with ambition to succeed, and she encouraged Jack to take a job at the H.C. Pitney General Store in Tampico in 1906. This was also to get Jack away from the influence of his older brother, who would eventually drink himself to death.

Nelle and Jack shared a love of theater, and in Tampico they formed a small dramatic group that staged plays at the Opera House. On a good night, they drew as many as a hundred people. Their first son, John Neil, was born in Tampico on September 16, 1908, and was forever known as "Moon." He made his stage debut at the Opera House as a dying infant in *The Dust of the Earth*. In Dixon, the family of four attended movies together on Friday nights.

From his mother, Ronald Reagan learned discipline, faith, tolerance, and a delight in performing. Following Nelle's lifelong practice, he continued to tithe (give 10 percent of his income) weekly to the Hollywood Beverly-Christian Church during his Warner Bros. years and long after he reached the White House. From his father, Reagan inherited charm, wit, and a gift for storytelling.

ABOVE: The Reagan family around 1913. Young Dutch was two, and his brother Moon was four.

Reagan and his mother Nelle at his triumphant 1950 Dixon homecoming.

FAITH

Jack Reagan was a gifted salesman and a good man, but he was cursed with a weakness for drink. Nelle sought solace in religion and in 1910 was received into the Christian Church of Tampico. The Christian Church, better known as the Disciples of Christ, opposed alcohol and abortion but was exceptionally tolerant on matters of race and encouraged women in the ministry. After the Reagan family settled in Dixon, Nelle became one of the Dixon Christian Church's most active and beloved members. She was also well known for her dramatic readings.

Years later, when the widowed Nelle, the proud mother of a movie star, was living comfortably in West Hollywood, she continued to devote herself to God's work. She visited the sick in hospitals and soul-sick convicts in prison.

Nelle's faith sustained them all during the bad times, and when Ronald Wilson Reagan took the presidential oath of office in 1981 and 1985, the Bible he used was Nelle's, open to her favorite passage, 2 Chronicles 7:14: "If my people, which are called by my name, shall humble themselves and pray, and seek my face, and turn from their wicked ways, then will I hear from heaven, and will forgive their sins, and will heal their land." Next to it, Reagan himself had written, "A most wonderful verse for the healing of the nation."

When Dutch was nine, the Reagans arrived in Dixon, on the Rock River in Illinois. With a population of ten thousand, it was ten times larger than Tampico, with several bustling factories and a thriving downtown. A new opportunity—a promised partnership in the Fashion Boot Shop—brought them to Dixon. The Reagan family's first home there was a rented white frame house with a modest front porch at 816 South Hennepin Avenue, close to downtown. Dixon was Ronald Reagan's hometown from age nine until twenty-one, and he would return to it throughout his life. At the Dixon Public Library he devoured tales of King Arthur and the Knights of the Round Table, the Rover Boys, Tarzan, Sherlock Holmes, and Horatio Alger.

Dutch was eleven years old when he first had to face up to his father's drinking problem. Until then, his mother or big brother had been around to look after Jack, and Dutch had the privilege of pretending to sleep.

But one winter's night the boy came home to find his father flat on his back on the front porch, drunk and dead to the world. There was no one to help him but Dutch, and Dutch would have much preferred to slip into the house, go to bed, and pretend he wasn't there. Yet he felt himself fill with grief for his father at the same time he was feeling sorry for himself. He said later, "Seeing his arms spread out as if they were crucified—as indeed he was—his hair soaked with melting snow, snoring as he breathed …, I bent over him, smelling the sharp odor of the speakeasy. I got a fistful of his overcoat. Opening the door, I managed to drag him inside and get him to bed."

At a young age, Dutch was forced to see his father's weakness and to demonstrate compassion. It is worth noting that this event occurred during Prohibition. The Eighteenth Amendment, which was passed the same year the Reagans arrived in Dixon, outlawed alcoholic beverages, but even the power of the federal government could not stop Jack Reagan and millions of others from drinking. It was young Dutch's first lesson in the futility of well-intentioned federally funded social programs.

A Love of God

Nelle Reagan was a teetotaler, a devout member of the Christian Church (Disciples of Christ) who vigorously supported Prohibition. As much as she despised drinking, however, she counseled her sons to "hate the sin but love the sinner," and to continue to love and honor their father in spite of his weakness. She instilled in her sons the belief that God has a plan for each of us, and therefore everything in life happened for a reason. It was a belief that would sustain Reagan throughout his life.

Nelle had joined the Christian Church of Dixon even before the family arrived in town, while the congregation was still meeting in the basement of the YMCA. She helped raise funds for a new building, and on June 21, 1922, Dutch and Moon were the first to be baptized there. For Dutch, the full-immersion baptism, meant to symbolize the death, burial, and resurrection of Christ, was a vivid experience. As the minister

intoned, "Arise and walk in the newness of faith," eleven-year-old Dutch invited Christ into his life.

Dutch attended church services on Sundays and Wednesdays, Sunday school, and, when he hit his teenage years, the Sunday evening youth group Christian Endeavor. By that time, Dutch was teaching a Sunday school class himself, bringing the Bible to life with his dramatic delivery.

Even far from Dixon and his childhood, Reagan's family ties remained strong. In his early years in Hollywood, he helped his brother get bit parts in the movies. Here, the brothers discuss a Hollywood script.

"Heroes Are More Fun"

In Dixon, Dutch Reagan's life revolved around church, school, and sports, not necessarily in that order. Jack Reagan was a fervent sports lover and was proud of his older son's achievements at sports-oriented South Dixon High School. Dutch went to the far more academically and artistically oriented North Dixon High School, but the two schools shared such things as sports teams and graduation ceremonies. Moon was the natural athlete of the family and excelled at all sports. Young Dutch lagged behind, which left him feeling inferior and yearning for self-confidence. He was always the last to be chosen for any game. No one realized at the time that he could barely see. He was finally

As a lifeguard at Lowell Park during the summer of 1927, Dutch Reagan was credited with saving seventy-seven lives from the treacherous Rock River.

Because Jack's income was never steady, Dutch and his brother were expected to help out. But they never pitied themselves. "We didn't know we were poor because the people around us were of the same circumstance," Reagan insisted years later. He caddied at the local golf course, and at fourteen he was working in construction during the summer and banking the money so he could go to college.

The one sport he excelled at was swimming, and in 1926 he became one of the first lifeguards at nearby Lowell Park. This was no easy job. The swift and winding currents of the Rock River could be treacherous because of an unexpected undertow, and the river had already claimed several lives the summer Reagan became a lifeguard there. He worked twelve hours a day, seven days a week, and he loved every minute of it. "You know why I had so much fun at it?" he later said. "Because I was the only one up there on the guard stand. It was like a stage. Everyone had to look at me." The children loved him, and years later they recalled how he made each one of them feel special.

By that time, Reagan had come into his own physically. The shy, undersize kid had matured into a tall, robust, and very handsome young man with a love of performing. He was president of the high school dramatics club, and he and his girlfriend, Margaret Cleaver, had the leads in Philip Barry's *You and I*. They performed in a one-act play, *The Pipe of Peace*, for the Dixon Women's Club, and appeared together in George Bernard Shaw's *Captain Applejack*, in which Dutch got to play a villain. "I learned that heroes are more fun," he said.

By senior year he had been elected president of his class and had filled out enough to play football for the varsity team. He also started as a center for the YMCA basketball team.

Throughout his life, Dutch firmly believed that playing sports built character and squelched racial bias. He was convinced that

fitted with thick horn-rimmed glasses at age thirteen. He hated wearing them, but being able to see clearly opened up a whole new world.

Dutch Reagan (back row, first on the right) continued to pursue his interest in theatre with The Dramatics Society at Eureka College.

no one who had played on a team of mixed races (as he had in high school and college) could ever be a bigot.

Because Jack could be unreliable and did not always understand his younger son's ambitions, Dutch found a second father figure in his minister, the Reverend Ben Cleaver. It was Cleaver, the father of Dutch's high school sweetheart, Margaret, who advised him about getting into college and even taught him how to drive a car.

Reagan also sought advice from B.H. Shaw, publisher of the *Dixon Evening Telegraph*, and a friend, drugstore magnate Charles Walgreen. Walgreen purchased Hazelwood, his estate on the Rock River, in 1928, and Reagan was often there during his college years as a caddie for Walgreen.

"The time never lies heavily upon him; it is impossible for him to be alone."

—Caption below Ronald Reagan's picture in the Eureka College yearbook, *The Prism*, 1932

He's Working His Way Through College

In September 1928, Dutch headed for Eureka College, one hundred miles from Dixon. Cleaver had encouraged him to choose Eureka, which was run by the Disciples of Christ. It appealed to Reagan because Margaret was planning to attend and because a

Reagan (front row, third from left) was a member of Teke fraternity in college.

boyhood football hero, Garland Waggoner, had played for Eureka's Golden Tornadoes. Hard-pressed as Nelle and Jack Reagan were, they supported their son's decision to go to college, although they could not help him financially. Cleaver arranged for a scholarship that paid half of Reagan's $180-a-year tuition and board. He earned the rest by washing dishes at his fraternity house, Tau Kappa Epsilon (Teke), and the girls' dormitory.

Situated on a lovely 114-acre campus, with towering red brick buildings and leafy, rolling terrain, Eureka had been founded by members of the Christian Church in 1855. It served the sons and daughters of the small towns and farms in surrounding counties,

and while the student body was rather small, it was not without academic distinction.

Reagan arrived just as the small college faced a financial crisis. Shortly before Thanksgiving, the school's president, Bert Wilson, announced faculty cutbacks and consolidations. There were rumors that he planned to cut the entire sports program. Students, urged on by the faculty and backed by the alumni, rallied at midnight in the college chapel to protest Wilson's moves. Reagan was chosen to present the plan to strike because he was a freshman, and with four years at Eureka ahead of him, he and his class had the most at stake.

Addressing that crowd of angry students was a thrilling experience for Reagan. For the first time in his life, he felt his words reach out and grab an audience. It was exhilarating. The crowd greeted every sentence with a roar, and after a while, it was as if he and the audience were one.

At Eureka, Reagan also found another father figure, the school's longtime football coach, Ralph McKinzie, and earned four letters playing football with the Golden Tornadoes.

Dark Days

Reagan's four years at Eureka coincided with the dawn of the Great Depression, the worst economic catastrophe the United States had ever seen. The stock market crash of 1929 was far removed from Dixon and Eureka, but the fallout hit them directly. The economy reached its nadir in 1932–33. *The Oxford History of the American People* said about the Depression, "The business world seemed to be crumbling everywhere; communists were full of glee over the imminent collapse of representative government and the capitalist system."

The Reagan family had never paid much attention to politics. All they knew was that they were worse off than ever. Jack had lost his stake in the Fashion Boot Shop in 1929, and Nelle was sewing in a dress shop for fourteen dollars a week. The only work Jack could get was managing a small, seedy shoe store in Springfield, two hundred miles from Dixon. He and the boys were home for Christmas Eve, 1931, when a special delivery letter arrived informing him that he had been fired. Things got so desperate in the new year that Nelle had to write to Dutch at school for help. To protect his father's pride, Dutch secretly sent her fifty dollars to keep the family going.

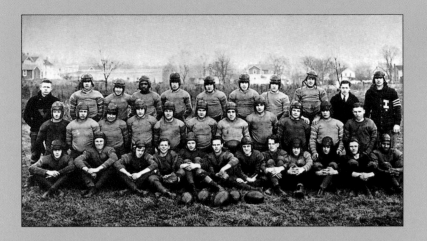

Both the Dixon High School football team (top) and the Eureka College football team (bottom) were racially integrated. Coincidentally, Reagan is fourth from left in the front row of both pictures.

TOLERANCE AND OPENNESS

Nelle and Jack shared a complete lack of prejudice and despised bigotry in others. Jack told his sons that once, on the road, he chose to sleep in his car rather than check into a hotel where the owner assured him they did not allow Jews.

When Dutch brought home his high school football team, he knew that his black teammates would be as welcome as the others. During Reagan's last semester of college, when Eureka's Golden Tornadoes were on a road trip and stopped near Dixon, the hotel refused to allow the team's two black players to spend the night. Reagan immediately suggested that they come home with him, where they were welcomed by Nelle and Jack.

Franklin Delano Roosevelt remained a lifelong influence on Ronald Reagan.

The New Deal in the Reagan Household

The New Deal brought the first measure of prosperity to the Reagan household. Jack had always been the ultimate outsider: an Irish Catholic in a Protestant town, a drinker in a world of teetotalers, a fervent Democrat among Republican loyalists. The New Deal turned his life around: after FDR's election in 1932, Jack was put in charge of the local Works Progress Administration to distribute food and jobs.

Dutch was proud of his father's contribution to the national recovery. The men Jack was putting to work were neighbors and the fathers of people he'd grown up with. Because of Jack, parks were created out of brush and swamp, and new bridges linked small towns and farms.

In these desperate days, the Reagan family and millions of other Americans found a hero, a visionary who promised to lead them out of the darkness. He was Franklin Delano Roosevelt, and like millions of other struggling Americans, the Reagans were convinced that he was the only man who could save the country.

Unemployed and a lifelong Democrat in a Republican stronghold, Jack Reagan worked hard as a volunteer to elect FDR in 1932. Newly graduated from Eureka and spending his last summer as a lifeguard at Lowell Park, Dutch proudly wore a "Win with Roosevelt" button on his swimsuit.

FDR promised "a new deal for the American people," and his followers marched to the voting booth to the tune of "Happy Days Are Here Again." Dutch Reagan was one of them and he cast his first presidential vote, for FDR, that November.

On the Radio

As hopeful as the Reagans were, Dutch knew he had to find a real job once Lowell Park closed that Labor Day. He dreamed of becoming a professional actor, but such a glamorous career seemed too far removed to be realistic for him. He turned to radio, which had just been introduced in 1920. Like any son of the Midwest, he initially headed for Chicago, his first visit since childhood. But Reagan was never a city man, and the size and the hectic pace were a shock. He had no contacts at the big radio stations and mostly got the brush-off until a kind receptionist at NBC suggested that he might have better luck breaking in if he were in a smaller city. Reagan was soon on his way to Davenport, Iowa, sixty miles from Dixon.

He was immediately hired at WOC—"where the West begins, in the state where the tall corn grows"—because he impressed the

During college, Reagan learned to love speaking to an audience. Not long after graduation, he combined his love of sports and his speaking ability to become a radio sports announcer, the Voice of the Chicago Cubs. Reagan was usually nowhere near the games he broadcast. He recreated them from reports relayed by a telegraph operator. He loved to recall the time the line went dead during a Cubs-Cardinals game, and he had to improvise for almost seven minutes.

management with his ability to re-create a sports game on the microphone. Just as immediately, he was fired because he fumbled while he read commercials. He was rehired only when his potential replacement insisted on a contract.

Dutch was soon making one hundred dollars a month, enough to send money home to his parents and to Moon, who was still at Eureka College. He was also paying off his college loan and tithing to his church.

On March 4, 1933, FDR—the president the Reagans had helped elect—took the oath of office and began his inaugural address with a trumpet call: "First of all, let me assert my firm belief that the only thing we have to fear is fear itself—nameless, unreasoning, unjustified terror which paralyzes needed efforts to convert retreat into advance." On March 12, FDR gave the first of his fireside chats, bringing his message to the American people via the radio on Sunday nights. He was the first president to use mass communications in this way and was a powerful influence on the young Ronald Reagan, who was about to move into big-time radio himself.

Bright Lights, Big City

The owner of WOC also owned WHO in Des Moines, and in the spring of 1933 he consolidated the two stations. Reagan, the up-and-coming sports announcer, moved to the much bigger city at twice his old salary. With a population of more than 140,000, Des Moines was an important stop on promotional tours. Celebrities like boxer Max Baer, movie stars Leslie Howard and James Cagney, and evangelist Aimee Semple McPherson all dropped by WHO to chat with Reagan. Des Moines native Joy Hodges, who had found fame as an actress/singer in the movies, would later play a key role in helping Dutch break into the movies. His smooth,

warm voice went out over fifty thousand watts of power on a clear channel to the small towns and farms of the Midwest, where he was fast becoming the well-known voice of Big Ten football and Major League Baseball.

He had expected to share all this with Margaret Cleaver when she returned from a graduation trip to Europe, but she told him in a letter that she had decided to marry a man she had met on her trip. She had been Reagan's girlfriend throughout high school and college, and he had truly expected that they would spend the rest of their lives together. He rebounded, however, and in Des Moines he began to enjoy the life of a handsome, young, single man-about-town with a glamorous job and money for the first time in his life.

He spent many nights with the WHO gang and his Teke fraternity brothers at Cy's Moonlight Inn, where the drink of choice was near beer, a nonalcoholic drink, spiked with a bit of bootleg whiskey. Even after Prohibition was repealed at the end of 1933, Reagan was never much of a drinker. One bad hangover was enough to get him to stick to moderation: "I decided if that's what you get for drinking—a sense of helplessness—I didn't want any part of it." He preferred to dance and spent many hours on the dance floor.

Reagan also took up horseback riding, something a poor boy could only dream about in Dixon. A friend told him that if he enlisted as a reserve officer in the 14th Cavalry Regiment at nearby Fort Dodge, he would be able to ride. His phenomenal ability to memorize helped him to pass the eye test, and he was commissioned a second lieutenant in the reserves. Riding would become a lifelong passion.

In 1937 Dutch Reagan was on top of the world that he knew, but he had not let go of his long-term acting dream. So when a chance came to see Hollywood, he was on his way.

Dapper and handsome, as a young man, Reagan was a swinger on the dance floor and an up-and-comer on the radio.

Chapter Two

HOORAY FOR HOLLYWOOD

1937–1941

"No one 'goes Hollywood'—they were that way before they came here. Hollywood just exposes it."

—Ronald Reagan, *People* magazine, February 9, 1987

onald Reagan's Hollywood career almost ended before it began. He walked out on his first screen test.

With typical caution, he approached his first visit to California as a business trip. Officially, he was traveling with the Chicago Cubs to their winter training camp on Catalina Island. But all along he planned to look up his new contacts in the movie business. One good friend, actress/singer Joy Hodges, generously

PAGE 22: Although Reagan was a handsome and popular movie star, he never forgot his humble roots in the Midwest. ABOVE: Warner had their new leading man posing for publicity stills even before he had seen his first script. Although this early photograph casts Reagan in a glamorous light, as a contract player he was wearing a suit he had brought with him from Des Moines. RIGHT: In *Love Is on the Air* (1937) Reagan played a battling broadcaster demoted to hosting a children's show. Notice that he was still wearing his wristwatch broadcaster style, with the face turned inward, so that he could keep track of the time. It became a lifelong habit.

Demonstrating a movie star's physique, Reagan posed for a sculpture class in 1940. The University of Southern California Division of Fine Arts had chosen him as a "Twentieth-Century Adonis."

offered to put him in touch with her agent, George Ward of the well-connected Meikeljohn Agency. Ward agreed with Hodges that the young sportscaster was exactly the likable, clean-cut American type that so many of the movie studios were looking for. He immediately scheduled a screen test for Dutch Reagan at Paramount.

The test was scheduled for early morning and Dutch was committed to broadcast a Cubs exhibition game that afternoon. The studio executives kept him waiting for an hour and finally said that they might not get to him until late afternoon. His course was clear. A paying job took priority over some highly speculative audition. Reagan walked out.

Fortunately, Ward had already arranged a second test at Warner. Dutch showed up for that one, gave it his best work, then took a train home to Des Moines.

On his first day back at WHO, he was handed a telegram from Meikeljohn: WARNER'S OFFER CONTRACT SEVEN YEARS, ONE YEAR'S OPTIONS STARTING AT $200 A WEEK. WHAT SHALL I DO? MEIKELJOHN

Reagan responded immediately: HAVE JUST DONE A CHILDISH TRICK. SIGN BEFORE THEY CHANGE THEIR MINDS. The "childish trick" was to leave town after the screen test. It worked. "Hollywood just loves people who don't need Hollywood," he said.

Dutch's Des Moines pals threw him a farewell party at the Moonlight Inn, after which he packed his three suits and headed for the movie capital behind the wheel of a new Nash convertible.

At Home in Hollywood

Reagan was about to join the busiest, most successful studio in Hollywood. According to an article in the December 1937 issue of *Fortune*, "Warner is the only major studio that seems to know or care what is going on in America besides pearl-handled gunplay, sexual dalliance, and the giving of topcoats to comedy butlers." With such stars under contract as Dick Powell, Pat O'Brien, Bette Davis, James Cagney, Olivia de Havilland, and Spencer Tracy, the studio was turning out an incredible sixty pictures a year. Their large 135-acre Burbank lot was considered the very best-equipped in Hollywood.

When Reagan showed up for work at Warner on June 1, 1937, he learned that he had already been cast in a movie that was to begin shooting the following Monday. Warner also intended to

change his name. Studio executives did not like the sound of "Dutch Reagan," the name he had answered to since childhood. While they tossed around different alternatives as if he weren't sitting there, Reagan finally spoke up and suggested the perfectly fine name he'd been born with. Thus it was agreed: Warner's newest leading man could call himself Ronald Reagan.

For his debut role in *Love Is on the Air* (1937), Reagan played a small-town radio announcer not unlike himself. In fact, the first time he saw himself onscreen, he was a little disappointed. Up there on the screen was plain old Dutch Reagan, and for him it was "one hell of a letdown."

The native midwesterner soon discovered that he loved California, the Sunshine State. He shared his impressions in a series of

Reagan's first screen role, in *Love Is on the Air* (1937), was close to his off-screen character: a brash headline-making radio personality who battles corrupt city officials. His leading lady was June Travis.

ABOVE: Reagan (center) had fifth billing as a drunken playboy hopelessly in love with Bette Davis in the critically acclaimed *Dark Victory* (1939). Director Edmund Goulding told him that he was playing the kind of man who could sit in the girls' dressing room dishing the dirt while they went on dressing in front of him. "I had no trouble seeing *him* in that role," said Reagan, "but for myself, I want to think I can stroll through where the girls are short of clothes, and there will be a great scurrying about and taking to cover." OPPOSITE: Swimming remained Reagan's favorite form of exercise.

articles he wrote for the *Des Moines Register*. He described the beauty of a California sunrise and what it was like to dine in fancy restaurants that offered exotic appetizers and plates heaped high "with bits of ham, pickled fish, spiced meats and goodness knows what else." He was honest enough to admit that he kind of liked it. After such a meal, he told the folks back home, "You feel so comfortable that you purr like a cat and don't give a whoop."

He told his readers that Hollywood was so full of astonishing wonders that you came to accept even the most ridiculous things as a matter of course. Yes, it could be a tough racket, but when you considered the rewards you were shooting at—fame and dizzying wealth—it was worth the chance you had to take.

Reagan was quickly getting an education in the eccentricities of the motion picture business. Six days after completing *Love Is on*

the Air, he was driving up the as-yet-unpaved Highway 1 to San Francisco to start shooting his second starring role, in *Sergeant Murphy* (1938), at the Presidio. He played a U.S. Cavalry private; the sergeant was a horse.

In rapid succession, Reagan filmed smaller parts in *Hollywood Hotel* (1937), a Busby Berkeley musical with Dick Powell, and *Swing Your Lady* (1938), which starred another up-and-coming actor, Humphrey Bogart. He was not billed in *Hollywood Hotel*, but

The cadets line up in this still from *Brother Rat*. From the bottom: Eddie Albert, who became the breakout star of the picture, Reagan, and Wayne Morris, whose own role had been expanded for the movie. Reagan and Morris would often be rivals for the same roles.

ABOVE: A poster for *Brother Rat*, a lighthearted look at the lives of first-year military-school cadets, features Jane Wyman and Reagan. OPPOSITE: Reagan and Wyman met on the set of *Brother Rat* (1938). By late 1939 they were engaged. Wyman, already an active member of the Screen Actors Guild, got Reagan involved in the union. When she was asked to serve as an alternate on the SAG board, Wyman recommended her husband instead. "He might even become president of SAG one day—or maybe America," she said.

one of the stars, powerful entertainment columnist Louella Parsons, who played herself, was delighted to learn that the young actor hailed from her hometown, Dixon, Illinois. She took a shine to the newcomer and became one of his most enthusiastic and influential supporters.

He also filmed *Submarine D-1* (1937) with Pat O'Brien but was cut from the final print. His character was supposed to come in at the end of the picture as the new fiancé of the female lead, but the studio dropped the idea, preferring that she remain faithful to the memory of her husband, who had been killed in a submarine accident. This ending emphasized the dedication of naval officers and their families to the service.

When Warner picked up his six-month option, Reagan felt secure enough to send for his parents to join him in California. He rented a modest apartment for them in West Hollywood, where the ailing Jack could take short walks. The studio added Jack to the payroll to handle his son's burgeoning fan mail. Nelle enrolled in the nearby Hollywood-Beverly Christian Church, and Reagan regularly attended services with her. He also tithed.

Reagan was discovering that in many ways Hollywood was just another small town. Service organizations were always on the lookout for volunteers with enthusiasm and leadership skills.

Reagan and Wyman filed a notice in Los Angeles of their intention to marry.

Thus, in 1938, he was recruited to be a director of the Screen Actors Guild (SAG), a union formed five years earlier to give performers more clout in dealing with the all-powerful studios.

In years to come, Reagan's work with SAG would make him a virtual spokesman for the entertainment industry. It would also give him a priceless education in the organized labor movement and communist attempts to influence mass communications.

Between 1939 and 1940, Reagan played a character called Bass Bancroft in a series of four action films inspired by the memoirs of a retired U.S. Treasury agent. In the first episode, *Secret Service of the Air*, Bass infiltrates a criminal ring that is smuggling illegal immigrants from Mexico into the United States. This was quickly followed by *Code of the Secret Service*, in which Bass battles coun-

terfeiters. *Film Daily* called it "a rip-roaring thriller of bare-fisted, walloping action." The following year, Bass battled counterfeiters again in *Smashing the Money Ring*, and in *Murder in the Air* he guards a new superweapon that could make the United States the greatest force for world peace ever.

Although never accused of being a Method actor, Reagan was always serious about preparing for a role. He spent a few weeks of intense training for the Bass Bancroft movies with a former junior welterweight world champion, Mush Callahan. The studio estimated that in the first three Bass Bancroft pictures, Reagan averaged one fight for every thousand feet of film.

The Bass Bancroft series also marked the onset of Reagan's hearing problems. On the set of *Secret Service of the Air*, someone fired a blank .38 cartridge too close to his right ear. It left him with a permanent hearing loss that would worsen later in life.

Reagan appeared in small roles in a few films that went on to become classics. In *Dark Victory* (1939) he played Bette Davis' playboy confidant (Humphrey Bogart was briefly seen as a stable hand). Later on, he would appear in *Knute Rockne, All American* (1940), *International Squadron* (1941), and *Desperate Journey* (1942).

It was clear that Warner was grooming Reagan for big things, and that meant publicity. They assigned him to escort the glamorous Lana Turner to the premiere of *Jezebel* (1938), which starred Bette Davis and Henry Fonda, and studio publicists tried to promote the idea that Reagan and Turner were a couple.

On his own time, Reagan preferred leading ladies of a quieter variety, like Joy Hodges and June Travis, his costar in *Love Is on the Air*. Both women shared his midwestern roots and traditional values. Each would eventually abandon her movie career for a fulfilling marriage.

Reagan and his leading lady of the moment enjoyed Hollywood's nightlife at clubs like Ciro's. Sundays were for horseback riding. At twenty-seven, he was ready to settle down with the right girl, and when he started filming his ninth picture, *Brother Rat* (1938), he thought he had found her. Today *Brother Rat* is best remembered as the film debut of Eddie Albert and the beginning of the offscreen romance between Ronald Reagan and the actress Jane Wyman.

Boy Meets Girl

By the time the former Sara Jane Fulks was cast in *Brother Rat*, the pert blonde with the large soulful eyes had spent nearly a decade knocking around Hollywood, working steadily in bit parts, usually cast as a dumb blonde or chorus girl. Unlike Reagan, who arrived in town with a contract, she had never had the security of a studio behind her until she signed with Warner in 1936. The studio immediately changed her name to Jane Wyman.

Wyman was in the process of an amicable divorce when she started filming *Brother Rat*, a comedy about three cadets at the Virginia Military Institute. Like so many others, Wyman was drawn to Reagan by his geniality and kindness. However, based on her experiences in Hollywood, she had to question whether these traits were authentic. "I couldn't help wondering if some of his easy good nature could be an act," she later candidly admitted.

The fairy tale marriage between Reagan, the All-American hero, and Wyman, a spunky, independent modern woman, was natural material for the fan magazines, and the couple gave many at-home interviews.

Newlyweds Mr. and Mrs. Ronald Reagan, just married at the Wee Kirk O'Heather Church, January 26, 1940. The powerful Hollywood columnist Louella Parsons hosted their wedding reception.

on Parade." (The tour had barely begun when Reagan's easy disposition was severely tested. A chartered plane was to take the group from San Francisco to Philadelphia. They flew all night through a blinding snowstorm until they were forced down in Chicago, from which they boarded trains. That was Reagan's first flight, and he refused to fly again for the next thirty-five years.) His outward serenity and unfailing good humor made a great impression on Jane. "For the first time in my life," she said, "I trusted someone."

On their return to Hollywood, Louella Parsons announced their engagement. The couple was married on January 26, 1940, at the Wee Kirk O'Heather Church in Glendale by Reagan's pastor from the Hollywood-Beverly Christian Church. Louella gave them a wedding reception, and after a brief honeymoon in Palm Springs, they moved into Jane's Beverly Hills apartment.

"It didn't seem possible that a man could have so easy a disposition consistently."

The Reagan-Wyman romance heated up considerably in late 1939, when Louella Parsons took them along on a nine-city, coast-to-coast vaudeville tour billed as "Hollywood Stars of 1940

Reagan and Wyman and baby Maureen Elizabeth made three.

The studio made the most of the wholesome, handsome young couple by immediately teaming them in *Brother Rat and a Baby* (1940). This sequel to *Brother Rat* reunited most of the cast, including the beautiful Jane Bryan, who was expected to become the next Bette Davis. Her new fiancé, businessman Justin Dart, would become a friend and mentor to Reagan and a member of his kitchen cabinet, an informal group of political advisers. Like the future Nancy Reagan, Bryan opted for marriage over a film career.

During the first year of their marriage, Reagan and Wyman were also teamed in *An Angel from Texas* (1940) and *Tugboat Annie*

As part of the star-making process, actors posed for endless publicity stills that were intended to establish their character. In Reagan's case, that was a natural, All-American leading man.

Sails Again (1940), which featured Neil (Moon) Reagan in a small part as one of penniless sailor Ronald Reagan's shipmates. Neither Wyman nor Reagan was considered a star. They were featured players making $500 a week. "I wasn't a glamour girl and he wasn't a matinee idol," she later recalled. "We were just two kids trying to get the breaks in pictures."

The newlyweds shared a commitment to their careers, a love of golf, and traditional liberal values. As avid golfers, they applied to the Lakeside Country Club, not far from Warner's studio. They were accepted, but when Reagan learned that studio head Jack Warner's application had been turned down because he was Jewish, he and Jane immediately resigned. They chose to golf instead at the Hillcrest Club, where Justin Dart and Dick Powell were members. Powell and Dart, both Republicans, would often argue politics with Reagan, but he remained steadfast in his loyalty to FDR, the New Deal, and the Democratic Party.

Becoming the Gipper

Easygoing Reagan was inclined to accept the roles the studio handed him, but Wyman understood that an actor had to go after the meatier parts that would bring him attention. When the newlyweds read in *Variety* that Warner planned to film *Knute Rockne, All-American* and was looking for an actor to portray Rockne's most famous player, George Gipp, they recognized a part that could have been written with Reagan in mind.

Pat O'Brien had already been cast in the title role of Notre Dame's legendary football coach. He had worked with Reagan on *Submarine D-1, Boy Meets Girl* (1938), and *The Cowboy from Brooklyn* (1938) and was happy to put in a good word for his young friend. Producer Hal Wallis was not so sure. He considered

Scene from *Knute Rockne, All American* (1940). "The Gipper only occupied one reel of the picture, but from an actor's point of view, it was a perfect part," Reagan recalled: "A great entrance, action in the middle and a death scene in the great tradition of Hollywood." It was an early example of how dogged Reagan could be when he wanted something.

Reagan "a hick radio announcer" until Reagan brought in some old photographs of himself playing football for Eureka's Golden Tornadoes.

Knute Rockne, All American turned out to be one of Reagan's most memorable films. He got to play a classic death scene, in which he whispers to Coach Rockne, "Someday, when the team's up against it, breaks are beating the boys, ask them to go in there with all they've got. Win one for the Gipper." (This powerful scene had to be cut from the television version for legal reasons. It is, however, available on the home video.)

Moviemaking was fast-paced at Warner where, as Reagan said, "They didn't want it fast, they wanted it Thursday." After completing *Knute Rockne, All American*, Reagan started filming another A-picture, *Santa Fe Trail* (1940), opposite Errol Flynn. This was his only Western for Warner. Reagan played the young George Custer, pursuing abolitionist John Brown (Raymond Massey), with Flynn as Jeb Stuart. The film also starred Olivia de Havilland, who would later become a SAG ally of Reagan's.

Reagan emerged from filming *Santa Fe Trail* just in time to begin plans for the gala premiere of *Knute Rockne, All American* in South Bend, Indiana. It was an event that marked a high point in his career and a chance to share his success with his ailing father.

"Here was an Irishman who had really worshiped from afar," Reagan recalled. "He'd never seen a Notre Dame team play. He thought Pat O'Brien was the greatest man since Al Smith." However, as much as Reagan wanted to share the big event with his dad, he hesitated. The family had lived too long in fear of what they called "the black curse"—Jack's drinking problem. Filial loyalty won out, however, and he invited his father to join him for the big event. And what an event it was. Stars like Bob Hope, Rudy Vallee, Anita Louise, and Rosemary Lane poured into South Bend for the two-day celebration. Beloved radio personality Kate Smith moved her weekly show to town for the occasion.

Much to his son's delight, Jack Reagan, a failed small-town shoe salesman, and Pat O'Brien, a movie star, bonded like two guys from the old neighborhood. After the October 4 premiere, most of the Warner party, including Reagan and Wyman, went back to their hotel to turn in. But Jack and Pat were just getting started. They spent the night carousing and returned to the hotel to join the group for early-morning services at Knute Rockne's grave.

Everyone capped off the celebration by going to the stadium to watch the Fighting Irish play the College of the Pacific. Reagan even got to broadcast the first quarter before they had to race to catch their train back to California.

Variety hailed *Knute Rockne, All American* as "an inspirational reminder of what this country stands for." It became Reagan's most successful film to date and a personal favorite.

Many years later, Reagan returned to Notre Dame as President of the United States to deliver the commencement address. Recalling the film, he told the new graduates that the picture was about more than a great coach who taught young men how to play a game well; it was about values. Knute Rockne's greatness lay in his belief that "the noblest work of man was molding the character of man." Four decades after filming Rockne's story, Reagan still considered him a powerful symbol of American virtues.

Beyond Hollywood

The year 1940 had been Reagan's best yet, and 1941 promised to be even better. Like most Americans, he was barely aware of the series of events in Europe and Asia that would change his world.

The Great War, the one that President Woodrow Wilson called "the war to end wars," had ended in 1918. Reagan, then seven years old, remembered the celebrations and the fact that some of the doughboys, infantrymen, he had watched march off to that war never returned. Like most Americans, he never expected the United States to become involved in such a calamity again.

But in Germany, Adolf Hitler was on the rise, and in the fall of 1936 he and Benito Mussolini formed the Axis alliance. By 1939, Hitler had invaded Austria and Czechoslovakia, Mussolini had seized Albania, and the Japanese had captured Shanghai.

In August, the Western world was shocked by the news that Joseph Stalin and Hitler, who had been at odds for years, had

His friend Pat O'Brien, who had been cast in the title role in *Knute Rockne, All-American*, helped Reagan lobby for the role of the Gipper. "There are other actors who could have done better," Reagan said at the movie's premiere, "But none wanted to do the part more than I."

REAGAN AND ROCKNE

For Ronald Reagan, *Knute Rockne, All American* was always about more than football. For him, the story of Rockne and the Gipper was all about sports and family and what schools like Eureka and Notre Dame and great coaches like Knute Rockne and his own beloved Ralph "Mac" McKinzie could do for a poor boy with nothing going for him but a willingness to work hard and dream big.

Reagan loved the equality of sports, and the fact that all that mattered on the playing field was how well one performed. He loved the bonding between players that happened on a well-coached team. He was proud that his high school and college teams were integrated in a time when movie theaters and hotels were not. His teammates were his friends, and he was convinced that no one who had played sports the way he had could emerge with prejudice against anyone.

Like the men who played football for Knute Rockne and Mac McKinzie, those who were privileged to work with Ronald Reagan in the Oval Office treasure the time they spent with one of the greatest coaches of all time.

shaken hands in a nonaggression pact. Only later would it be revealed that part of the deal was an agreement to partition a conquered Poland.

Hitler launched his attack on Poland on September 1, 1939. Two days later, Great Britain and France declared war on Germany. World War II was on. Stalin soon annexed Finland and three Baltic states: Latvia, Estonia, and Lithuania. In April 1940, Germany moved into Denmark and then Norway. In May Germany invaded neutral Belgium and Holland, under cover of Luftwaffe bombs. In June, Paris fell. In September, Japan formally joined Germany and Italy in an agreement that if any one of the three went to war with the United States, the others would join in.

Across the Atlantic, only England remained free, as the Luftwaffe generals mounted a furious air assault on London and other cities. British Prime Minister Winston Churchill stood brave, defiant, and alone. The question now was not if, but when the United States would enter the war.

Like most Americans in 1941, however, Reagan was more concerned with his home, his job, and his community than events in far-off lands. Jane gave birth to their first child, Maureen Elizabeth, on January 4, 1941, her own twenty-seventh birthday. She and Reagan began plans to build a dream house in the hills above Sunset Boulevard. His thoughts were occupied with a new baby, a new home, and a new direction for his career.

Going Places

Reagan was working constantly, switching easily from light comedy to drama. Warner loaned him out to MGM for *The Bad Man* (1941), a Western with Wallace Beery and Lionel Barrymore. Beery played a Mexican bandit on whose loyalty a former friend,

played by Barrymore, must depend. Reagan's character, Barrymore's nephew, had once saved the outlaw's life. His uncle is about to lose the family ranch when Beery turns up to pay off his debt. Reagan had little chance against these two veteran scene-stealers. He later complained that Barrymore, who was confined to a wheelchair, used to deliberately run over his feet.

Back at Warner in *Million Dollar Baby* (1941), a romantic comedy, Reagan was teamed with Priscilla Lane as a poor but proud pianist troubled by his girlfriend's sudden fortune. *Nine Lives Are Not Enough* (1941) followed. The fast-paced whodunit drew praise from *Variety*: "Ronald Reagan is not only a brash reporter to end all reporters, he's also hilariously scatterbrained and devilishly resourceful…. Reagan gives a superbly helter-skelter performance."

Next, Warner cast him in *International Squadron (1941)*, one of a number of anti-Nazi movies being produced by the studio at the time. Reagan played an American who joins the Royal Air Force and dies in combat.

Soon thereafter, the studio decided that their rising young contract player was ready for a major role in a major film, a quantum leap from anything he'd done before.

Kings Row

Kings Row (1942) was based on writer Henry Bellamann's gloomy bestseller about sinister events in a small town. Screenwriters and the Production Code Administration (which made sure all that

OPPOSITE: "Where's the rest of me?" Reagan asks Ann Sheridan in *Kings Row*. He regarded this as one of his favorite roles, and this particular scene as the most challenging of his acting career. He was able to deliver it in one take. "I had put myself, as best I could, in the body of another fellow." Still, it was so powerful and grim that it was almost cut from the final version.

SHARING THE LIMELIGHT

Reagan's Hollywood career gave him plenty of experience coping with the challenges he would face as President. During his second term, the nation had entered an era of prosperity that would continue into the 1990s. Credit for this economic recovery often went to Federal Banking chief Paul Volcker. Reagan was once asked if he felt upstaged by Volcker. "Oh, no," he said, "I once played opposite Errol Flynn."

"I became the Errol Flynn of the Bs [B-pictures]," Reagan said of himself. " I was as brave as Errol, but in low-budget pictures." The top movie still shows Reagan, Flynn, and Arthur Kennedy in *Desperate Journey*. The bottom one features Flynn, Alan Hale, and Reagan in the same movie.

Few believed that the controversial bestselling novel *Kings Row*, with its themes of incest, insanity, euthanasia, mercy-killing, and more, in a small town, could ever be filmed. But an only slightly sanitized version of the book provided Reagan with one of the most memorable roles of his career. He called it the performance he was most proud of. *Kings Row* was nominated for three Academy Awards: Best Cinematography (James Wong Howe), Best Director (Sam Wood), and Best Picture (Hal B. Wallis).

appeared onscreen was appropriate for viewing) whittled out most of the themes of incest, nymphomania, mental illness, and euthanasia, leaving the key role of Drake McHugh at the center of the story. Reagan was not Warner's first choice for the role, nor even its second. But when Dennis Morgan, Franchot Tone, Fred MacMurray, Ray Milland, Lew Ayres, Robert Preston, and Eddie Albert all proved unavailable, Reagan got the part. He played a small-town rake whose legs are amputated after a freight-car accident. He awakens in an upstairs bedroom to utter the heartbreaking line, "Where's the rest of me?" It was Reagan's first experience with an acting chore that "got down inside and wrung me out," and it left such an impression on him that years later, he chose the line for the title of his first autobiography.

Always interested in new technology, Reagan was fitted with contact lenses while filming *Kings Row* and encouraged other actors to give them a try.

When Reagan finished filming at the end of the summer, he had no doubt that he had done his best work so far. He expected his performance to draw major attention once it was released. He was on the brink of a major step forward in his career. Meanwhile, he took a break for a Dixon-style homecoming.

Homecoming

September 10, 1941, was officially Louella Parsons Day in Dixon. The famous columnist and native daughter had been invited back, and she suggested that Reagan also be invited. Warner was happy to turn the event into a premiere for his latest release, *International Squadron*. As their train pulled into Dixon, there was no doubt that the crowd had turned out for Reagan.

The spirit of isolationism still reigned in the Midwest. The countries that had already fallen to the Axis powers seemed very far away. But among the celebrity guests Warner brought in were Bebe Daniels and Ben Lyon and their infant son, who were a living reminder that there was a war on in Europe. Daniels and Lyon could speak firsthand about the London bombings. For the last two years, they had been broadcasting their weekly show in London, remaining on the air while bombs went off around them.

Daniels and Lyon joined in the triumphant parade honoring Parsons and Reagan. There were outdoor dinners nightly on the Walgreen estate and a ball at the Dixon armory. "Here were a one-time five-dollar-a-week reporter and a lifeguard who achieved what Dixon and all 100-percent hero-worshiping Americans dream of," said the *Chicago American*. Hooray for Hollywood indeed.

Reagan's lifelong passion for horses began in Des Moines. In spite of his poor eyesight, he managed to enlist in the U.S. Cavalry Reserve, mainly for the training in horsemanship, at Fort Dodge. Until then, he admitted, all he knew about horses came from watching Tom Mix movies.

Chapter Three

A CITIZEN POLITICIAN

1941–1964

"As a citizen I would not like to see any political party outlawed on the basis of its political ideology."

—Ronald Reagan, testimony before the House Un-American Activities Committee, 1947

Returning to Hollywood from his triumph in Dixon, Reagan continued on his lucky streak. He plunged into filming *Juke Girl* (1942), a well-intentioned drama about migrant workers that costarred Ann Sheridan. His agent, Lew Wasserman of MCA, had already capitalized on the anticipated success of *Kings Row* to negotiate a landmark new contract that tripled Reagan's salary and guaranteed him $1 million over a seven-year period. Only later would Reagan realize that he had also joined the 91 percent tax bracket, which began his hatred for taxes. For now, Reagan had every reason to believe he was a man who had it made. Then overnight, the world changed.

On December 7, 1941, the Japanese bombed Pearl Harbor, the U.S. naval base in Hawaii. The next morning, Reagan and millions of other Americans awoke to the news that thousands of American servicemen and civilians had been killed or wounded, and over one hundred planes had been destroyed on the ground or in the water. The *USS Arizona* had been destroyed, the *Oklahoma* had been shattered and capsized, four other battleships were resting on the bottom or run aground to prevent sinking, two naval auxiliaries had been destroyed, and three destroyers and

ABOVE: Second Lieutenant Ronald Reagan, U.S. Army Cavalry Reserve, reported for duty in April 1942. He was honorably discharged with the rank of Captain in late 1943. OPPOSITE: Originally, Reagan was cast to star opposite Ann Sheridan in *Casablanca* (1942). By the time filming began, however, Reagan was in the Army, and the leads would be Humphrey Bogart, Paul Henreid, and Ingrid Bergman. PAGE 42: As president of the Screen Actors Guild, Ronald Reagan listened to testimony about possible communist activity in the entertainment world in October 1947, at a session of the House Un-American Activities Committee investigation in Washington. He knew he would be testifying the next day.

a few other vessels had been badly damaged. More devastating hits followed in Formosa, Manila, the Malay Peninsula, and Guam.

Twenty-four hours after this unprovoked attack, a furious Franklin D. Roosevelt addressed Congress and declared December 7 "a day that will live in infamy." Before the day was over, the House and Senate had voted to declare war on Japan. With the exception of one negative, the vote was unanimous. Germany and Italy, Japan's partners, then declared war on the United States. Reagan, an active member of the U.S. Cavalry Reserve since his days in Des Moines, was not surprised when he was called to serve.

Warner requested and received an extension long enough for him to complete *Desperate Journey* with Errol Flynn. A spirited drama of American bomber pilots stranded in Germany, it gave Reagan the chance to battle the Nazis figuratively. A high point came for him when, he said, "I knocked an arrogant Gestapo officer. . . and calmly helped myself to his breakfast."

This Is the Army

In April 1942, Second Lieutenant Ronald Wilson Reagan reported for active duty at Fort Mason in San Francisco. He had been

On the set of *This Is the Army* (1943) with Joan Leslie. The movie was based on a hit Broadway musical with book, music, and lyrics by Irving Berlin. Reagan, like other stars in the service, was paid only his Army wages. Warner Brothers turned over all profits to Army Emergency Relief.

blind as a bat most of his life and had worn thick eyeglasses since the age of thirteen. At thirty-one, he was nearly deaf in his right ear since the accident on the set of *Secret Service of the Air*, the father of a one-year-old child, and the sole support of his widowed mother. Nevertheless, he was eager to serve.

His Warner salary was suspended the day he went on active duty. Jane was back at work, and her income provided for herself and Maureen, but Reagan regarded his mother's support as his responsibility. He took a loan from the studio to provide for her and agreed to repay it when he returned to civilian life.

Reagan's induction physical confirmed that his eyesight was terrible. One examining physician told him, "If we send you overseas, you'll shoot a general," to which another doctor added, "Yes, and you'd miss him."

Reagan was assigned to be a personnel officer in the First Motion Picture Unit (FMPU), stationed at Fort Roach in Culver City, near Hollywood. The FMPU made training films and prepared aerial photographers for combat camera crews.

The unit's most important job was also its most secret. FMPU special effects men, all Hollywood veterans, built a complete miniature of the city of Tokyo that covered most of the floor space of a soundstage. Above this they rigged a crane and a camera mount to photograph the miniature city, giving the effect on screen of movies taken from a plane traveling at any height and speed. It provided American pilots with a dress rehearsal before they bombed Tokyo.

It was typical of Reagan to immerse himself in all aspects of the experience, from the technical to the humanitarian. He read all the narratives of Medal of Honor winners that came across his desk and was deeply affected by these accounts of heroism. For him, these were the things that America was all about.

Reagan bristled at the suggestion that anyone in the FMPU was avoiding combat. "The army doesn't play that way," he insisted. "There was a special job the army wanted done and it was after men who could do that job. The overwhelming majority of men and officers serving at our post were limited service like myself." Like many others who did not experience combat, he had an almost reverent feeling for those who did.

At Fort Roach, Reagan also had his first encounter with the civil service bureaucracy. As the base personnel officer, he wanted to lay off certain civilian employees he considered incompetent or simply unnecessary. He was prohibited from doing so by civil service regulations, and he did not like it.

Reagan narrated morale films like *Rear Gunner* (1942), which was also released commercially. He appeared in a joint Army-Warner effort, *This Is the Army* (1943), an Irving Berlin musical with George Murphy, Joe Louis, and Kate Smith, among others. Reagan was promoted to first lieutenant in October.

The Passing of FDR

The war was virtually over with the Allied victory in 1945. That February an ailing FDR traveled to Yalta in the Crimea to meet with Churchill and Stalin to agree on the terms of Germany's surrender. The Soviet Union emerged with a number of concessions,

In a publicity still from *This Is the Army*, Reagan lunches with a fellow actor.

First Lt. Reagan pauses to sign autographs for fans.

many of them secret, that would not long after sow the seeds of the Cold War. The events at Yalta would have a profound effect on Reagan's view of Communism in general and Soviet tactics in particular.

On April 12, two months after Yalta, FDR passed away. The official announcement was that death had come suddenly of a cerebral hemorrhage. Only a few insiders were aware that he had been failing for months.

Millions of Americans, including Reagan, mourned the passing of a man they had only just reelected to an unprecedented fourth term. This patrician with the common touch had become president during the nation's worst depression and had given citizens like the struggling Reagan family a reason to hold on to the American dream. FDR's career and leadership style would continue to influence Reagan long after he left the Democratic Party behind.

When Ronnie Comes Marching Home

In July, newly promoted Captain Reagan was discharged. He was eager to return to his old life. He and Jane had adopted a baby boy, Michael, on March 18, 1945. In *Where's the Rest of Me?* he wrote, "All I wanted was to rest up a while, make love to my wife and come up refreshed to a better job in an ideal world. (As it came out, I was disappointed in all these postwar ambitions.)" The world he was returning to as a civilian had changed profoundly. To begin with, both his marriage and his acting career were in deep trouble.

For years, Jane Wyman had yearned to play serious dramatic roles while Warner continued to cast her in lightweight romantic comedies. Her big break came in 1944, when she was loaned out to Paramount for *The Lost Weekend*, with Ray Milland. It was a stark, unsparing portrayal of a man's descent into alcoholism, and Jane had a small but important part as the woman who loves but cannot save him. Both stars were best known for romantic comedies, but under the direction of Billy Wilder they established themselves as serious actors. The following year, *The Lost Weekend* swept the Academy Awards, garnering Oscars for Best Picture, Best Director, Best Actor, and Best Screenplay. Jane had to be satisfied with critical acclaim for her supporting role.

Encouraged, she followed *The Lost Weekend* with *The Yearling* (1947), the sensitive tale of a young boy and a deer. This time out, she was nominated for Best Actress, and Reagan was at her side at the Academy Awards ceremonies to console her when she lost to Olivia de Havilland (*To Each His Own*).

Jane was pregnant that night and due in September. Reagan told reporters that they might name the baby Oscar because "Jane deserves one around the house." Alas, she lost the baby, one more event in what would turn out to be a devastating year.

Reagan agreed to film *That Hagen Girl* (1947) with Shirley Temple only because Jack Warner pressured him. With a baby due in four months, he could not afford to go on suspension. The movie was supposed to help child star Temple, who was now nineteen, make the transition to adult roles. Instead, it seriously damaged both stars' careers.

George Murphy (in the dark suit) played Reagan's father in *This Is the Army* Offscreen, Murphy, a successful stage musical comedy star who made the transition to films, became a role model for Reagan. Raised as a Democrat, in 1939 he had switched to the Republican party, and in 1943 he was elected vice president of SAG. Later Murphy would serve as president of SAG and then be elected to the U.S. Senate by the voters of California.

THE GRADUATE

Twenty-five years after his graduation, Ronald Reagan returned to Eureka College as its most famous graduate and delivered the 1957 commencement speech. In it, he recalled how the Great Depression affected the struggling midwestern college during the four years he spent there, and how grateful he was for the chance at an education. His speech was notable not only for his eloquence and passion, but for the fact that in it he set forth the principles that would dominate his political career. Here are some excerpts:

Even with study and reading I don't think you can quite understand what it was like to live in an America where the Illinois National Guard, with fixed bayonets, paraded down Michigan Avenue in Chicago as a warning to the more than half million unemployed men who slept every night in alleys and doorways under newspapers. On this campus many of us came who brought not one cent to help this school and pay for our education. The college, of course, had suffered and lost much of its endowment in the stock crash, had seen its revenue, not only from endowment but from gifts, curtailed because of the great financial chaos. But we heard none of that. We attended a college that made it possible for us to attend regardless of our lack of means, that created jobs for us, so that we could eat and sleep, and that allowed us to defer our tuition and trusted that they could get paid some day long after we had gone. And the professors, God bless them, on this campus, the most dedicated group of men and women whom I have ever known, went long months without drawing any pay. Sometimes the college, with a donation of a little money or produce from a farm, would buy groceries and dole them out to the teachers to at least try and provide them with food.

Almost a century and a half after [the signing of the Declaration of Independence], this nation entered a great world conflict in Europe. Volumes of cynical words have been written about that war and our part in it. Our motives have been questioned and there has been talk of ulterior motives in high places, of world markets and balance of power. But all the words of all the cynics cannot erase the fact that millions of Americans sacrificed, fought and many died in the sincere and selfless belief that they were making the world safe for democracy and advancing the cause of freedom for all men.

A quarter of a century later America went into World War II, and never in the history of man had the issues of right and wrong been so clearly defined, so much so that it makes one question how anyone could have remained neutral. And again in the greatest mass undertaking the world has ever seen, America fulfilled her destiny....

And now today we find ourselves involved in another struggle, this time called a Cold War. This Cold War between great sovereign nations isn't really a new struggle at all. It is the oldest struggle of humankind, as old as man himself. This is a simple struggle between those of us who believe that man has the dignity and sacred right and the ability to choose and shape his own destiny and those who do not so believe. This irreconcilable conflict is between those who believe in the sanctity of individual freedom and those who believe in the supremacy of the state.

In a phase of this struggle not widely known, some of us came toe to toe with this enemy, this evil force, in our own community in Hollywood, and make no mistake about it, this is an evil force. Don't be deceived because you are not hearing the sound of gunfire, because even so you are fighting for your lives. And you're fighting against the best organized and the most capable enemy of freedom and of right and decency that has ever been abroad in the world....

We won our fight in Hollywood, cleared them out after seven long months in which even homes were broken*, months in which many of us carried arms that were granted us by the police, and in which policemen lived in our homes, guarding our children at night....

Now that the first flush of victory is over we in Hollywood find ourselves blessed with a newly developed social awareness. We have allowed ourselves to become a sort of village idiot on the fringe of the industrial scene, fair game for any demagogue or bigot who wants to stand up in the pulpit or platform and attack us. We are also fair game for those people, well-meaning though they may be, who believe that the answer to the world's ills is more government and more restraint and more regimentation. Suddenly we find that we are a group of second-class citizens subject to discriminatory taxation, government interference and harassment.

Remember that every government service, every offer of government-financed security, is paid for in the loss of personal freedom...in the days to come whenever a voice is raised telling you to let the government do it, analyze very carefully to see whether the suggested service is worth the personal freedom which you must forgo in return for such service.

*Editor's note: Reagan is not being ungrammatical here. He is probably thinking of the toll the battle took on his marriage to Jane Wyman.

One scene called for Reagan to rescue the girl from a frigid lake. The scene had to be shot a number of times, and five days later Reagan was hospitalized with pneumonia.

While he was isolated at Cedars of Lebanon Hospital, Jane was rushed to Queen of Angels in premature labor. On June 26, 1947, she gave birth to a girl who lived only twenty-four hours. Depressed by the loss of her baby, an ordeal she had been forced to go through alone because Reagan was still confined to the hospital, Jane was clearly at a crossroads in her life. She sought solace in her career and her most promising role yet.

Since seeing *Johnny Belinda* on Broadway years earlier, she had yearned to play the heroine, a deaf-mute rape victim. Warner paid a record $50,000 for the movie rights and cast Lew Ayres as a heroic doctor. Once Jane recovered, she went straight into filming the most important role of her life.

Fighting Communists in Hollywood

Unlike Wyman, Reagan was paying less and less attention to his movie career. He had rejoined the SAG board just as the actors' union was entering a critical decade.

Communists, gangsters, and labor leaders all saw the potential power of the entertainment industry and mass communications. A consequent struggle for power among technical unions led to a 1946 industry strike in which SAG remained neutral. The atmosphere outside the striking studios grew violent. Someone stabbed a picketer at Universal Studios. Demonstrators overturned automobiles at MGM and smashed windshields at Warner.

For protection, Warner brought in nonstriking workers by bus. Studio security advised Reagan to lie down to avoid rocks and Coke bottles. "I couldn't do that," he recalled. "So instead they

After the war, Reagan went back to acting. In *Storm Warning* (1951), he played a crusading D.A. in a small southern town who teams up with a visiting model, played by Ginger Rogers, to battle the Ku Klux Klan. Doris Day had a rare non-singing role.

made me sit by myself. They figured that if I was going to get it nobody else would be hurt."

But security was no laughing matter. In October, while filming a beach scene for *Night Unto Night* (1949), Reagan heard from an anonymous caller who said that if he gave his antistrike report to the SAG members, a "squad" would disfigure him so that he would never make films again. The studio took the threat seriously enough to arm him with a .32 Smith and Wesson.

The battle for power in Hollywood between the communists and the anticommunists was very real. In 1920 Vladimir Lenin, founder of the Soviet state, declared, "Morality is entirely subordinate to the interests of class war. Everything is moral that is necessary for the annihilation of the old exploiting social order and for uniting the proletariat."

The United States had just emerged from a war in which the motion picture industry had played a key role in maintaining national morale and overcoming America's traditional isolationism. Communist control of motion picture production would give them control of the world's most efficient propaganda machine. Such plans did not escape the attention of Congress, which had established the House Un-American Activities Committee (HUAC) to investigate "communist infiltration of the motion picture industry," among other forms of mass media.

Frightened studios and television networks observed a blacklist of writers and directors who had belonged to certain leftist groups or who had merely refused to answer some of the HUAC's questions. These people could no longer get work in the film industry.

Reagan resisted what he called "unofficial blacklists," but he was determined to fight the efforts of communist organizations to grab power in the film industry. In the fall of 1947, Reagan himself was subpoenaed to appear before the committee.

Reagan was no admirer of the HUAC. He detested big government as much as he detested communism, and he believed that the HUAC had no business encroaching on the rights of private citizens. He told them as much when he testified in Washington on October 25. They asked him what steps he recommended to rid the motion picture industry of communist influences. "I think within the bounds of our democratic rights, and never once stepping over the rights given us by democracy, we have done a pretty good job in our business of keeping these people's activities cur-

tailed," he said. "After all, we must recognize them at present as a political party. On that basis we have opposed their propaganda, and I can certainly testify that in the case of the Screen Actors Guild, we have been eminently successful in preventing them from, with their usual tactics, trying to run an organization with a well-organized minority."

Reagan still considered himself a liberal and made no apologies for it. He might not agree with the Communist Party members in his profession, but he would defend their right to their views. He resented what he regarded as their underhanded methods and dishonest tactics for trying to gain control of SAG. He deeply distrusted their efforts to use the power of the movies for propaganda.

ABOVE: This emergency meeting of the SAG board, on October 3, 1946, was attended by Reagan (top) and other board members, including, from left: Henry Fonda, Boris Karloff, and Gene Kelly. OPPOSITE: Reagan testified before HUAC about Communist Party efforts to control the film business. Reagan assured the committee that "the best thing to do is to make democracy work. In the Screen Actors Guild we make it work by ensuring everyone a vote and by keeping everyone informed."

Reagan went on to tell the HUAC, "I would say in opposing these people that the best thing to do is to make democracy work. In the Screen Actors Guild we make it work by ensuring everyone a vote and by keeping everyone informed. I believe that, as Thomas Jefferson put it, if all the American people know all of the facts they will never make a mistake."

Membership in the Communist Party was not illegal at that time and Reagan made it clear he did not support the idea of outlawing it in the future: "As a citizen, I would hesitate or not like to see any political party outlawed on the basis of its political ideology. We have spent 170 years in this country on the basis that democracy is strong enough to stand up and fight against the inroads of any ideology."

HUAC chairman J. Parnel Thomas and other members were impressed with Reagan's testimony, but he had one more point to make: "I detest, I abhor their philosophy, but I detest more than that their tactics, which are those of the fifth column, and are dishonest, but at the same time, I never as a citizen want to see our country become urged, by either fear or resentment of this group, that we ever compromise any of our democratic principles through that fear or resentment. I still think that democracy can do it."

The Lone Ranger

While Reagan was testifying before the HUAC, *Johnny Belinda* (1948) had opened and Wyman's virtuoso performance was being acclaimed. In January she was nominated for an Academy Award, but the newly separated Reagans attended the ceremony independently. Jane accepted her Oscar with the shortest speech on record: "I accept this very gratefully for keeping my mouth shut. I think I'll do it again."

By all accounts, Reagan had been stunned when Wyman asked for a divorce and clung to the hope that they could reconcile. "It's a very strange girl I'm married to, but I love her," he said. "I know we will end our lives together." But Wyman had made up her mind. "In recent months," she told the judge, "my husband and I engaged in continual arguments on his political views; finally there was nothing left to sustain the marriage."

Reagan did not contest the divorce, but all who knew him in those days remember that he was devastated. "I suppose there had been warning signs," he acknowledged. "If only I hadn't been so busy, but small-town boys grow up thinking only other people get a divorce. The plain truth was that such a thing was so far from even being imagined by me that I had no resources to call upon."

The dream house on the hill was sold. Jane moved with the children to a new home in Malibu. When the divorce was final, on July 16, 1948, she was in England making *Stage Fright* for Alfred Hitchcock. Reagan was at her house looking after the young Maureen and Michael.

Ironically, he proceeded to put in some of his best work in a series of romantic comedies: *The Voice of the Turtle* (1948) with Eleanor Parker, *John Loves Mary* (1949) with Patricia Neal, and *The Girl from Jones Beach* (1949) with Virginia Mayo. Though newly single, he was not interested in chasing girls. "He was a guy looking for companionship more than anything else," said friend Eddie Bracken.

OPPOSITE: In the movie *Law and Order* (1953), Reagan plays a marshal who just wants to settle down and live quietly in the town of Cottonwood. But some folks have other ideas. *Law and Order* seemed to bring out the worst in later political opponents, beginning with Governor Edmund "Pat" Brown, who used a clip from the film in a campaign commercial, "A Man Against the Actor." In it Reagan's character warns: "You wanted law and order in this town, you've got it. I'll shoot the first man that starts for those steps."

A Hurting Heart

In November, Reagan sailed to England to film *The Hasty Heart* (1949) with Richard Todd and Patricia Neal. It was his first trip abroad and he spent four lonely months in London while the city, still suffering the deprivations of the war, was shrouded in its worst fog in a hundred years. He also learned on arrival that he was the second lead and believed that once again the studio had misled him.

Things got even worse when Reagan came home and broke his leg in three places during a charity softball game. He was hospitalized for eight weeks and did not work for months. He had to turn down two pictures and lost $150,000 in potential income. No one from the studio called him until it was time for him to promote *The Girl from Jones Beach*.

In January 1950 an uncharacteristically glum Reagan told columnist Bob Thomas, "After spending most of the last year in bed, I'm going to concentrate on my career in 1950." He was

ABOVE: This is a rare photograph of Reagan on a tractor. Although he hailed from farm country, he never claimed to have spent any time working on a farm. Even on his beloved ranch, he was more concerned with clearing flammable brush and chopping wood than planting crops. OPPOSITE: In 1945 Reagan had signed a seven-year, million-dollar contract and he felt on top of the world. But he was never able to reestablish the prewar momentum of his acting career.

working on his first postaccident picture, *Storm Warning* (1951), a serious drama about important social issues in which a fashion model (Ginger Rogers) arrives in a small southern town to visit her sister (Doris Day) and witnesses a Ku Klux Klan murder. Reagan, as a crusading attorney, got to call the Klan "a bunch of hoodlums dressed up in sheets," a line that would have made his Klan-hating father proud.

In general, Reagan was not pleased with the scripts Warner was offering him. "I'm going to pick my own pictures," Reagan told Thomas. "I have come to the conclusion that I could do as good a job at picking as the studio has done. At least I could do no worse." He even hinted that he might go back to broadcasting. Studio head Jack Warner was not amused when he read Reagan's remarks. Everyone knew that most of Reagan's pictures had been made for Warner, and Jack took it as a direct criticism.

However, Reagan had a point. He had gone ahead with *That Hagen Girl* when even studio executives admitted that it was not a good script. Jack Warner had talked him into it by promising that if he brought in a good Western, Warner would make it. Reagan did bring in a good Western, *Rocky Mountain* (1950), and the studio made it—with Errol Flynn.

In the middle of all this, Reagan got his first break since returning to civilian life: a young woman in distress. She considered herself to be in danger and was convinced that he was the man who could help her.

A Damsel in Distress

Nancy Davis arrived in Hollywood when she was twenty-eight. She won a contract at MGM and was cast in a series of small parts playing a wholesome wife and mother. Her first starring role was in *The Next Voice You Hear* (1950), with James Whitmore, which

drew wonderful reviews but failed at the box office. By the time she was cast as George Murphy's wife in *Talk About a Stranger* (which eventually appeared in 1952), Nancy knew her days at MGM were numbered.

Her most immediate problem was that she was receiving mail from left-wing organizations that was meant for another Nancy Davis, a bit player. She was concerned that someone might mistake her for a communist and that she would end up blacklisted. She brought her problem to director Mervyn LeRoy, who put her in touch with Reagan. He thought it was something SAG should look into.

Although she projected the air of a Chicago debutante, Davis' early life had been difficult. Born Anne Frances Robbins, abandoned by her father shortly after birth, she was raised by relatives while her mother, actress Edie Luckett, worked in theatre on the road.

Nancy was practically a teenager when her mother married Dr. Loyal Davis, a prominent Chicago surgeon. Nancy attended Smith College, where she acted in plays, and later tried to break into theatre in New York, with little success. Edie encouraged her interest in acting and gladly called on her friends in the movie business to help her little girl. One of them, Spencer Tracy, arranged a screen test for Nancy at MGM.

When Nancy filled out her questionnaire, she gave her "greatest ambition" as "to have a successful marriage." When asked if she had any particular phobias, she mentioned "superficiality. Vulgarity, especially in women. Untidiness of mind and person. And cigars."

OPPOSITE: Ronald Reagan and Nancy Davis made only one picture together, *Hellcats of the Navy* (1957). He played a World War II submarine commander, and she was the nurse in love with him.

Reagan agreed to discuss her problem over dinner with the proviso that it would be an early evening. That was fine with her—they both were working and had early calls. But they were soon deep in conversation, and he found himself opening up about his small ranch in the San Fernando Valley, his horses and their bloodlines, the Civil War, and his growing interest in wine. After dinner, they went to Sophie Tucker's opening at Ciro's and danced to the music of Xavier Cugat's band. They stayed for the second show and closed the place.

Soon Nancy was attending weekly SAG meetings, and Reagan discovered that she shared his interest in politics. Still, steady courtship was difficult. He traveled frequently on SAG business. On weekends, ten-year-old Maureen and five-year-old Michael joined him, and he and Nancy would pile them into his battered red station wagon and drive out to his new ranch in Lake Malibu.

He was still not ready to jump into marriage again. When Reagan returned to Des Moines and Dixon to promote *Louisa* (1950), the first of five pictures he had contracted with Universal,

OPPOSITE AND ABOVE: Reagan costarred with Walter Slezak and Diana Lynn in *Bedtime for Bonzo* (1951). Many jokes have been made about the film but it reflected traditional values that were important to Reagan. He plays a psychology professor convinced that environment, not heredity, determines a person's fate. The professor was raising a chimpanzee (Bonzo) as a human being to prove his theory. The role had some parallel to Reagan's own life: the professor wanted to prove that he was not destined for the penitentiary like his father; Reagan was determined not to be the failed dreamer his father was.

Ronald Reagan and Nancy Davis were married on March 4, 1952, in a simple but deeply meaningful ceremony to both of them. Fellow actors William and Ardis Holden were best man and matron of honor, respectively.

he traveled with his mother, Nelle. The picture remains memorable only because it marked the debut of the young Piper Laurie, who played his daughter.

Later that year, he made his second film for Universal, *Bedtime for Bonzo* (1951). He played a college professor determined to use a chimp to prove that nurture is more important than nature. The movie has been the target of much ridicule, mainly from people who never saw it, but America had monkeys on its mind in the early 1950s. (Cary Grant starred the following year in *Monkey Business* as a scientist who discovers a rejuvenating scrum that has him acting like a young chimp.)

Ronnie Loves Nancy

A lot had happened—and not happened—in the years since Reagan had signed his million-dollar contract. When it expired in January 1952, Warner chose not to renew it. After fifteen years of loyal service and cooperation, forty-one films without a single suspension, he left the Warner lot on January 28 without so much as a handshake from Jack Warner. Still, he remained optimistic. A month later, he asked Nancy Davis to be his wife.

They were married on March 4 at the Little Brown Church, a branch of the Christian Church that Reagan and his mother attended in the San Fernando Valley. Film star William Holden and his wife Ardis (who had been a leading lady under the name Brenda Marshall) were the best man and matron of honor. The newlyweds spent their wedding night at the Old Mission Inn at Riverside. The next day, they drove to Phoenix, Arizona, to celebrate with Nancy's mother and stepfather. Dr. Davis would become another profound influence on Reagan's political thinking and his gradual move to the Right.

By 1964, Reagan had grown from a handsome movie actor to a serious labor negotiator. The previous decade had been a tough one, and he was at a crossroads in his life.

Nancy gave birth to their first child, a daughter, Patricia Ann, on October 22. Reagan had just been hit with a whopping tax bill and had still not reestablished himself in the movies. He let his agents talk him into a two-week engagement in Las Vegas, where he emceed a revue at the Last Frontier Hotel. He opened there on February 15 and brought his trademark professionalism and good cheer to the experience. The show consisted of the Continentals, a male quartet; the Blackburn Twins, a song and dance act; and the Honey Brothers, a rough-and-tumble comedy team. In between the acts Reagan cracked jokes, and he joined the acts in some of their routines.

If he regarded Vegas as a comedown, he didn't show it. But inside Reagan knew the nightclub life was not for him. On his return to California, he told his agents that he would never again sell himself so short.

Reagan suspected that his activism as SAG president had hurt his image with the studios. "They stop thinking of you as an actor," he said. "The image they have of you isn't associated with your last role, but with the guy who sat across the conference table beefing. And that's death."

He began to consider television and, with it, the most important step of his life.

Bringing Good Things to Light

In September 1954, Reagan signed a deal with General Electric to host a weekly dramatic anthology and to represent the company as a spokesman. He would introduce each episode and sign off at the end with the words, "Here at General Electric, progress is our most important product." His contract called for him to appear in some episodes.

GE Theatre featured many of Hollywood's top stars; among those who made their television debuts on the show were Alan Ladd, Fred MacMurray, Bette Davis, and Joan Crawford. Nancy Davis Reagan and her husband appeared as a Native American couple in the November 23, 1958, episode, "A Turkey for the President."

What made the deal special, however, was the commitment to visit GE factories and offices. According to Nancy Reagan, during his eight years with GE, her husband spent a total of two years on the road. All told, he visited 135 plants and spoke to 250,000 employees. He usually met with workers in offices or on the factory floor and addressed them at shift changes, so he saw their working lives first-hand.

It was during these years that Reagan developed his technique of giving brief opening remarks about values and the country's problems, then shifting to taking questions. Unlike career politicians, he was getting a total immersion course in the concerns of working American men and women.

His companion on most of these visits was GE executive Earl Dunckel, who remembers that Reagan would spend the long travel hours reading newspapers, magazines, and books: "He would be making notes all the time. He'd scribble on cards; he'd underline articles." It was a habit Reagan would continue throughout his life, and one that would serve him well.

The GE experience was a happy one on every level. In 1956, when the Reagans built a new house in Pacific Palisades, GE provided them with state-of-the-art electrical appliances, turning it into a showplace with such up-to-the-minute innovations as an electric garbage disposal.

The GE contract also allowed Reagan to make the occasional film. In 1957, he and Nancy appeared in their only movie together, *Hellcats of the Navy*.

Fighting for the Union

In November 1959, Reagan was elected to an unprecedented sixth term as president of SAG. He was reluctant to take on the post again and was convinced that his reputation had suffered with producers who now saw him as an adversary. Nevertheless, it was an important time. SAG was on the verge of the first strike in its history. At stake was the question of actors' rights in the release of films to television.

In brief, movie theater attendance was plunging as postwar America stayed home to watch television. Producers were eager to sell their libraries of old films to the new medium, but they were not as eager to share the revenues with the actors. This disagreement led to long, hard negotiations between SAG and producers during the summer of 1958.

Reagan was a skilled negotiator who never took a confrontational position and was never dogmatic. Charlton Heston, a member of the negotiating committee, praised Reagan's role: "He might disagree, but he'd find a way to leave the other side with a feeling that they were good guys, too, and not the enemy. That is

The Reagans managed to maintain the devotion of honeymooners throughout their life together. "My life began when I married Ronnie," Nancy Reagan has said more than once, and her husband was just as devoted. "I can't imagine my life without her," he said. "Obviously, I'm very much in love with her."

As president of the Screen Actors Guild, Reagan was an important industry negotiator. As early as April 1949, he joined associates from other industry unions to petition the White House's help in aiding their members. From left: Roy M. Brewer, IATSE (International Alliance of Theatrical Stage Employees); Kenneth Thompson, SAG; Reagan; Richard Walsh, International President, IATSE.

Reagan's own agency, MCA, became the first to agree to pay actors residuals when television programs in which they performed were rebroadcast. Once MCA conceded, the other producers fell into line. "Every writer, actor and director in this town ought to get down and kiss Ronald Reagan's feet," one former MCA agent told author Ronald Brownstein, "because the man got television residuals. That has paid for most of the houses in the [San Fernando] Valley."

By now, however, Reagan's vision had moved beyond the entertainment industry and union politics. He was concerned about U.S. relations with the Soviet Union. In 1960 an American U-2 reconnaissance flight was shot down over Russia, giving Premier Nikita Khrushchev a temporary propaganda advantage in the Cold War. An invitation for President Dwight Eisenhower to visit the U.S.S.R. was withdrawn. The election of John F. Kennedy in 1960 only seemed to encourage more Soviet saber rattling.

In August 1961, two months after a seemingly successful meeting with Kennedy in Vienna, Khrushchev ordered construction of a concrete and barbed-wire wall dividing Berlin's eastern and western zones. Khrushchev intended to stem the flight of Germans from communist East Germany to democratic West Germany. The move violated all international agreements. The Western powers merely registered their protest.

This was followed a year later by the revelation that the Soviets were constructing new missile sites in Cuba. A showdown forced them to withdraw for the time being.

All this disturbed Ronald Reagan greatly.

Moving On

The year 1962 was one of major changes. Nelle Reagan passed away on July 25, and GE Theatre became a ratings casualty when *Bonanza* moved to Sunday nights. Reagan briefly moved on to host *Death Valley Days*, but he would not be able to resist the call to public service much longer.

That November, in an attempt at a political comeback, Richard Nixon was running for governor of California. Reagan was campaigning for him when a woman in the audience called out, "Mr. Reagan, are you still a Democrat?"

"Yes, ma'am, I am," he said.

"Well," she answered, "I'm a deputy registrar and I'd like to change that."

And she came right up on the stage and changed the lifelong Democrat's registration. Ronald Reagan was now officially a Republican.

Reagan made his last movie, *The Killers*, a Western with Angie Dickinson, in 1964. He was cast against type as a heavy and got good reviews, but his interests had changed. That October, he got a call that would transform his life forever. Senator Barry Goldwater was the Republican nominee for president and his campaign was in trouble. The election was weeks away and he desperately needed Reagan's help.

Reagan and Angie Dickinson starred in *The Killers* (1964), his last film, and the first and last time he played a villain. Based on a short story by Ernest Hemingway and directed by Don Siegel, it is today considered an underrated film noir.

Chapter Four

A Rendezvous with Destiny

1964–1980

"Already the hour is late. Government has laid its hand on health, housing, farming, industry, commerce, education, and to an ever-increasing degree interferes with the people's right to know....
We approach the point of no return when government becomes so huge and entrenched that we fear the consequenses of upheaval and just go along with it."

—Ronald Reagan, 1964

Ronald Reagan first stepped onto the national political stage on October 27, 1964, with a simple thirty-minute speech that would change history. He was there to help out the failing campaign of Republican presidential nominee Senator Barry Goldwater. Goldwater's advisers, who were very impressed by Reagan's fundraising ability in California, suggested taking his speech national. The senior senator from Arizona was in a bitter and doomed race against President Lyndon Johnson. Reagan acted out of friendship and conviction, never realizing that the speech would establish him as a powerful voice for traditional American values and a potential candidate for political office. Yet the speech almost didn't air because at the last minute Goldwater's advisers were worried that Reagan's message might be too controversial.

In her autobiography, *My Turn*, Nancy Reagan revealed that two days before the speech was supposed to air, Senator Goldwater called Reagan at home to say that his advisers wanted him to cancel the broadcast. "Have you read the speech?" Reagan asked. "No," said Goldwater, "but they tell me you've got something in there about Social Security." "That's true," Reagan acknowledged. "I said that any individual paying into Social Security should have a right to declare who his beneficiary should be." That seemed reasonable enough to Goldwater, but he asked to preview the film

Above: On January 4, 1966, with Nancy at his side, Reagan declared his candidacy for the Republican nomination for governor of California. He described himself as a "citizen politician." PAGE 66: In his inaugural address, Reagan cited Benjamin Franklin: "'If ever someone could take public office and bring to public office the teachings and the precepts of the Prince of Peace, he would revolutionize the world and men would be remembering him for a thousand years.'" Reagan promised to try to live up to that ideal.

of the speech just to be sure. When he finished, he ordered his staff to go ahead and air it.

Reagan's speech, called "A Time for Choosing" (pg. 70), echoed the same themes he had been putting forward for years on the factory floors of General Electric and at meetings in small-town community centers. He warned about the dangers of big government, the loss of individual liberty, and the erosion of traditional morality. He neither praised Goldwater nor denounced President Johnson. Instead, Reagan stuck to themes that struck a chord with Americans everywhere. "You and I have a rendezvous with destiny," he told them, echoing his onetime hero, Franklin D. Roosevelt. "We will preserve for our children this, the last best hope of man on earth, or we will sentence them to take the last step into a thousand years of darkness. If we fail at least let our children and our children's children say of us: we justified our brief moment here. We did all that could be done."

"The Right Thing for a Citizen to Do"

The reaction to Reagan's speech was immediate. At Goldwater's campaign headquarters in Washington, D.C., the telephone switchboard lit up with calls of support from those who had been stirred by Reagan's words. In time, his single speech would raise a

Barry Goldwater and Reagan were titans of the conservative movement. The rise of the movement from political obscurity in the 1940s to political power in the 1980s was chronicled in *The Conservatives*, a PBS documentary, in 1987. The program included personal reminiscences from (shown from left): Goldwater, Reagan, and the latter's longtime friend, William F. Buckley.

record-breaking $8 million for the Goldwater campaign. However, Reagan's efforts came too late to save the campaign entirely, and the senator went down to resounding defeat. President Johnson and Hubert H. Humphrey were elected by a landslide. Still, time would show that although the last soldiers of the New Deal had won this battle, they were losing the war.

After the election, the national Republican Party was in disarray. In California, party leaders recognized that the fresh, confident voice of Ronald Reagan offered them a potential candidate for public office. They approached him about running for governor. At first, he was not interested, but he was willing to think about it. He spent the last six months of 1965 traveling throughout California, making some speeches, and sharing ideas with people in the small towns and cities throughout the state. He learned that he had a lot of support among working people. It seemed to Reagan that his fellow Californians seriously wanted to reverse the

A Time for Choosing

The bitterness of the 1964 presidential campaign is long forgotten, but anyone today can read the text of Reagan's speech and marvel at his clarion call for all Americans to return to the traditional values that made our country great. His simple words are even more powerful more than thirty-five years after he delivered them. "A Time for Choosing" included the following:

The sponsor has been identified, but unlike most television programs, the performer hasn't been provided with a script. As a matter of fact, I have been permitted to choose my own words and discuss my own ideas regarding the choice that we face in the next few weeks. I have spent most of my life as a Democrat. I recently have seen fit to follow another course. I believe that the issues confronting us cross party lines. Now one side on this campaign has been telling us that the issue in this election is the maintenance of peace and prosperity. The line has been used: "We've never had it so good." But I have an uncomfortable feeling that this prosperity isn't something on which we can base our hopes for the future. No nation in history has ever survived a tax burden that reached a third of its national income. Today, thirty-seven cents out of every dollar earned in this country is the tax collector's share. And yet our government continues to spend seventeen million dollars a day more than the government takes in. We haven't balanced our budget twenty-eight out of the last thirty-four years. We've raised our debt limit three times in the last twelve months. And now our national debt is one and a half times bigger than all the combined debts of all the nations of the world. The trouble with our liberal friends isn't that they're ignorant. It's just that they know so much that isn't so.

I am going to talk of controversial things. I make no apology for this.... Those who deplore use of the terms "pink" and "leftist" are themselves guilty of branding all who oppose their liberalism as right-wing extremists. How long can we afford the luxury of this family fight when we are at war with the most dangerous enemies ever known to man? If we lose that war, and in so doing lose our freedom, it has been said history will record with the greatest astonishment that those who had the most to lose did the least to prevent its happening. The guns are silent in this war, but frontiers fall while those who should be warriors prefer neutrality....

If all of this seems like a great deal of trouble, think what's at stake. We are faced with the most evil enemy mankind has known in his long climb from the swamp to the stars.... We are being asked to buy our safety from the threat of the Bomb by selling into permanent slavery our fellow human beings enslaved behind the Iron Curtain. To tell them to give up their hope of freedom because we are ready to make a deal with their slavemasters....

You and I have a rendezvous with destiny. We will preserve for our children this, the last best hope of man on earth, or we will sentence them to take the last step into a thousand years of darkness.

In 1964, Reagan campaigned vigorously for Republican presidential candidate Barry Goldwater throughout California. Reagan's speech, "A Time for Choosing," won standing ovations everywhere, and in the last days of the failing campaign, he agreed to deliver it on network television. Although it could not save Goldwater, its effect on the party was electrifying, revitalizing the Republicans even as they faced sure defeat. Political columnist David Broder of *The Washington Post* hailed Reagan's appearance as "the most successful national political debut since William Jennings Bryan electrified the 1896 Democratic convention with his Cross of Gold speech." *Time* magazine called it "the one bright spot in a dismal campaign."

"So what's this empty nonsense I hear about Ronald Reagan being 'just an actor'? I watched Ronald work most of his adult life preparing for public service. His will be a new, informed, vigorously dedicated leadership. So on November 8, vote for Ronald Reagan."

— John Wayne, TV endorsement for Reagan's first campaign for governor

order of things. They were concerned that with more regulations and confiscatory taxes, the government was taking more of their money, more of their options, and more of their freedom.

Reagan was concerned about the state's future. Student protests, which had started in September 1964 with the free speech movement at the University of California at Berkeley, had spread to other campuses. Radical students were occupying university buildings and halting classes to protest escalating U.S. involvement in Vietnam. The race riots that had broken out in the Watts neighborhood of Los Angeles in 1965 had spread to other big cities. On the national front, Reagan was watching with growing concern as President Johnson increased the national debt and cut defense spending at the same time that U.S. conflicts with the Soviet Union increased and the commitment in Vietnam escalated. He worried that LBJ's Great Society programs meant a more powerful federal government at the expense of the states. The growing tax burden to support LBJ's Great Society was starting to take a toll on ordinary Americans.

"I went into politics in part to put up my hand and say, 'Stop,'" he later said. "I was a citizen-politician and it seemed the right thing for a citizen to do." By the end of the year, he had made up

his mind. On January 4, 1966, he announced that he would run for governor of California.

As a candidate for governor, Reagan was a complete outsider. At fifty-five years old, he had never held public office, and he wanted to run the second largest state in the Union. Reagan liked to point out that if California were a country, it would be the seventh largest economic power in the world. He was running as a Republican in a state where Democrats outnumbered Republicans three to two. He was challenging a popular two-term, incumbent governor, Edmund G. "Pat" Brown, who represented exactly the "progressive" big government that Reagan had come to deplore. Brown was proud that during his eight-year administration the state had build a vast system of freeways and expanded its fine state university system. He was also confident, having already defeated one famous challenger, former vice president Richard M. Nixon, and he was not impressed with Reagan. That was his first mistake. Governor Brown was the first opponent to underestimate Ronald Reagan, but he would not be the last.

At the beginning of the campaign, Brown attacked Reagan's lack of experience. But the affable Reagan turned that right around. "I don't know anybody who was born holding public office," he said. "The man who currently has the job has more political experience than anybody. That's why I'm running." Years later, Brown acknowledged that he enjoyed making fun of Reagan's Hollywood career. "I thought it was a joke—[the Republicans] running a motion picture actor," a still-bitter Brown said, "and he was not a grade-A actor." However, Reagan never thought he had to apologize for his movie career. He had always been proud to be a part of the motion picture industry and of his service in the Screen Actors Guild. In fact, Reagan made no apologies at all. He preferred to attack Governor Brown's record of big government handouts. He also managed to turn Brown's jibes into

Governor Reagan writes memos on his first day in office in Sacramento.

jokes and got in a few cracks of his own. When a reporter asked the former host of *Death Valley Days*, "Will you give Governor Brown equal TV time?" Reagan responded, "Well, sure, our audience is accustomed to seeing both ends of a horse."

Toward the end of the campaign, a desperate Governor Brown was captured on news footage talking to a group of black schoolchildren. "I'm running against an actor," he told them warmly, "and you know who shot Lincoln, don't you?" Reagan himself refused to believe the story until he actually saw the film. The actor won by nearly one million votes.

Back on the Late, Late Show

Reagan was sworn in as the thirty-third governor of California shortly after midnight on January 1, 1967. In the waning days of the Brown administration, the governor had been busy granting pardons and appointing as many as eight or ten new judges a day. Reagan was anxious to begin his own agenda as soon as possible.

That night, Ronald and Nancy arrived for the ceremony around midnight, after dining with friends. They were shocked to

In Reagan's first swearing-in as governor, on January 1, 1967, California State Supreme Court Justice Marshall F. McComb administered the oath of office and California Senate Chaplain, Rev. Wilbur W.Y. Choy, holding the Bible, gave a blessing.

be greeted by television lights, a choir, and a crowd of well-wishers, an unusual occurrence at that time. Among them was an old friend of Reagan's, fellow actor George Murphy, who had been elected to the U.S. Senate in 1964. Reagan had not prepared any kind of a speech, but he was suddenly asked to say a few words. He looked out at the crowd gathered on the capitol steps, turned to Senator Murphy, and said, "Well, George, here we are again on the Late, Late Show." The tension broke and he followed with a rallying inaugural speech. A new era had dawned in California.

Governor Reagan

Governor Reagan arrived in Sacramento with virtually one goal: to cut the size and cost of the state government. "We stand between the taxpayer and the tax spender," he declared. But once he got to work, Reagan discovered that for the last year the state had been spending $1 million a day more than it had been taking in. The previous administration had left him with a deficit of

Nancy Reagan tried to keep a brave face as she took a look at her new home in Sacramento. The grand old Victorian mansion had seen better days and she worried that it was a firetrap. She had given up a dream house in Pacific Palisades and their ranch in Malibu. Publicly, she insisted: "I could be happy anywhere if my husband and children are with me," but she soon found a more suitable residence, which the Reagans leased and paid for themselves.

nearly $200 million. Desperate measures were necessary. He was forced to sign the largest tax increase in California history. Once he overcame that hurdle, however, Reagan surprised veteran politicians by making his first term a success. He managed to reduce the size of California's welfare rolls and balance the state budget.

All the while he was establishing an excellent working relationship with the state legislature's entrenched Democratic old guard.

His years with SAG had honed his pragmatism when it came time to negotiate. He told supporters that if he could get 70 percent of what he wanted from a legislature controlled by the opposition, he would take his chances of getting the other 30 percent when they saw how well the first 70 percent worked.

However, Reagan took a much harder line with the student protestors who occupied buildings at the University of California at Berkeley. When the protestors started lobbing rocks and tear gas at the police who tried to evict them, Reagan did not hesitate to declare martial law. He sent in twenty-five hundred members of the National Guard to restore order. As a man who had washed dishes to put himself through college, Reagan had zero tolerance for campus demonstrators. "Their signs said, 'Make love, not war,' but they didn't look like they could do either," he remarked. At one meeting, a student got up to tell the governor candidly that it was impossible for people of his generation to understand young people. "You grew up in a different world," the student said. "Today we have television, jet planes, space travel, nuclear energy, computers...." When he paused for breath, Reagan said, "You're right. It's true we didn't have those things when we were young. We invented them." On another occasion, as the governor's limousine moved through a crowd of student demonstrators, a young man held up a sign reading "We are your future." Quick-witted Reagan hastily scribbled his own sign and held it against the car window: "I'll sell my bonds."

Fighting Vietnam

As for the escalating situation in Vietnam, Reagan was adamant. "We should declare war on Vietnam," he had said in October

1965. "We could pave the whole country and put parking stripes on it and still be home by Christmas."

He cared deeply about the American fighting forces serving in this controversial war. During his first term, he and Nancy gave four dinners for prisoners of war returning to California. Many of these men had survived years of brutal torture and harrowing conditions. Nancy recalled that one of the men would always propose a toast to the governor as thanks for his support. Reagan would always respond the same way: "No, we're here to thank you for what you've done for us."

The press often missed his private acts of kindness. Nancy recalled that a soldier from Sacramento who was fighting in Vietnam had sent the governor a money order and asked him to have flowers sent to his wife on their anniversary. The governor delivered them personally to the astonished woman.

In May 1967 he debated the issue of the Vietnam War with Senator Robert F. Kennedy on national television, and most viewers thought Reagan prevailed. A year later, minutes after winning the California primary, Kennedy was dead, cut down by an assassin's bullet, and the Democratic convention in Chicago that summer produced bloody riots in the streets. Thirty thousand Americans had been killed in Vietnam and the war had become a flash point at home.

Reagan with his two youngest children, Patti and Ron. After Patti published a controversial autobiographical novel in 1985 (*Home Front*), Reagan told Barbara Walters, "I thought I was a good father. Maybe there were times when I should have been sterner than I was."

A Wave Sweeping the Land

Reagan briefly considered making a run for the presidency in 1968. He told James Reston of *The New York Times*: "I am convinced that there is a wave sweeping the land that started in 1966. A wave of desire for a change, dissatisfaction on the part of the people over what's going on, a feeling that many of the programs that were born with such promise have not borne fruit." In a speech that year to the Economic Club in New York, he said, "I do not remember a time when so many Americans, regardless of their economic or social standing, have been so suspicious of the aims, the credibility, and the competence of the federal establishment. There is a question abroad in the land: 'What is happening to us?'" He led the California delegation to the Republican convention in Miami as its "favorite son." Support for him there demonstrated that he had a growing national constituency.

In the end, Reagan chose to finish out his term as governor and united with his fellow Republicans to nominate Richard Nixon. The politically reborn Nixon defeated Democrat Hubert Humphrey that November.

Governor Reagan's first term in Sacramento had brought some disappointments: he was forced to raise taxes to balance the state's budget, and he was unable to cut back the state's vast bureaucracy. The annual state budget more than doubled, topping $10 million. However, by the end of his first year in office, Reagan had begun to turn things around. The conservative newcomer had demon-

OPPOSITE: Reagan did not let his political ambitions interfere with his long friendship with the controversial Frank Sinatra. Like Reagan, Sinatra was a cradle Democrat, but he left the party after Hubert Humphrey's defeat in 1968. He soon lent his considerable support to Reagan's second campaign for governor of California.

strated that he could work effectively with a Democratic legislature to achieve what was best for California. (Reagan would demonstrate this ability again as president when he would work with a Democratic Congress and negotiate with the Soviet Union.) The voters appreciated Reagan and in 1970 elected him to a second term. Their faith was justified as his efforts began to pay off. Reagan was finally able to enact welfare reforms while spending more on elementary and secondary education than had his predecessor.

> *"When we start thinking of 'us' instead of 'them,' we've been in government too long."*
>
> — Ronald Reagan, declaring himself a canidate for the Republican presidential nimination, 1976

Entering the National Stage

President Nixon recognized Reagan's growing national support. In the fall of 1971, Nixon surprised many of his longtime supporters by establishing diplomatic relations with the communist People's Republic of China. In the controversy that followed, he asked Governor Reagan to fly to Taiwan to explain this enormous reversal in U.S. foreign policy to our friends the Nationalist Chinese and to reassure them about Nixon's pending visit to Peking the following February. The Governor and Mrs. Reagan also visited the Philippines and Vietnam on this trip. On their return they telephoned the families of every single serviceman they had met in Vietnam.

The Democratic Party that Reagan had grown up with was heading ever more to the Left. In 1972 it nominated George S.

McGovern to challenge President Nixon's bid for reelection. Nixon scored a phenomenal victory: 47,165,234 votes to McGovern's 29,710,774. Nixon racked up 520 electoral votes to McGovern's seventeen. But the second Nixon term was soon mired in scandal.

Reagan had always considered himself a "citizen-politican," not a career one. By 1974, at the end of his second term, he was looking forward to retreating to his ranch, a 688-acre spread in the

Reagan came to the campaign trail late in life, but he took to it immediately.

Santa Ynez Mountains northwest of Santa Barbara that he had dubbed Rancho del Cielo ("heavenly ranch"). However, once again, events in the outside world demanded his attention. In Washington the Watergate scandal was growing and President Nixon was right in the middle of it.

Reagan remained loyal to President Nixon until the very end. Only as Nixon was preparing to resign on August 9, 1974, did Reagan acknowledge that the president had deceived the country and Congress. Even then, Reagan did not join those demanding Nixon's resignation. He wanted Nixon to go before Congress and explain what had happened. Within three weeks of Nixon's resignation, and even before he was pardoned by his successor, Gerald Ford, Reagan was urging that Nixon not be prosecuted, saying, "The punishment of resignation certainly is more than adequate for the crime."

Running for the Only Job Tougher than Governor

Reagan had always honored the California Republicans' eleventh commandment: "Thou shalt not speak ill of another Republican." Nevertheless, some of President Ford's more liberal policies bothered Reagan greatly. He was concerned that Ford, a career legislator before Nixon appointed him as vice president, was part of the Washington establishment. "We need a government that is confident not of what it can do," he said, "but of what the people can do." He was also uneasy with Henry Kissinger's foreign policy, which Reagan believed was weakening American influence all over the world just when Soviet power was expanding. In 1976, Reagan decided to challenge President Ford's bid for a second term, and came very close to winning the Republican nomination.

Reagan had always reveled in the opportunity to meet people during his many trips for General Electric. He was anxious to hear their stories, their troubles, and their concerns. And they convinced him that he had enough grassroots support out there to sustain his first bid for elective office.

On the campaign trail, he addressed lingering bitterness about Vietnam: "Let us tell those who fought in that war that we will never again ask young men to fight and possibly die in a war our government is afraid to win." Reagan ran a good race in the primaries, easily besting Ford in North Carolina and Texas, but Ford had all the weapons of an incumbent president on his side. Reagan referred to this power at a North Carolina stop: "I understand Mr. Ford has arrived in the state," he said wryly. "If he comes here with the same lists of goodies he brought to Florida, the band won't know whether to play 'Hail to the Chief' or 'Santa Claus Is Coming to Town'."

By March, most Republican leaders, including Reagan's old friend Barry Goldwater, had endorsed President Ford. The local campaigns got rougher, and by the time of the California primary, the Ford campaign had produced a television commercial that ended with a warning: "When you vote Tuesday, remember

Governor Reagan couldn't start a war. President Reagan could." In this case the scare tactic backfired, and Reagan carried the state by a two-to-one margin.

Success on the campaign trail made his narrow loss at the Kansas City convention all the more painful. In a late-night convention roll call, the nomination went to incumbent Gerald Ford, who won on the first ballot by gaining 187 more votes than Reagan's 1,070. Ford named Senator Robert Dole of Kansas as his running mate.

Recognizing Reagan's growing importance, Ford invited him to address the gathering. In a stirring call for party unity, Reagan reminded his fellow Republicans that their concern must be with preserving individual freedom and saving the world from nuclear destruction, rather than with fighting among themselves. He reminded the delegates that they were all living in a world where the great powers possessed awesome missiles of destruction that could, in a matter of minutes, destroy the civilized world. He urged the convention delegates to go forth united, citing the words of General Douglas MacArthur: "There is no substitute for victory." Ford had won the nomination, but the applause that greeted Reagan that night made it clear that the Gipper had won their hearts. That November, President Ford was defeated by the Democratic candidate, James Earl Carter, the former governor of Georgia, and Carter's running mate, Senator Walter Mondale of Minnesota.

Since his first term as governor, people had been urging Reagan to run for president. In 1976 he announced that he would challenge incumbent Republican Gerald Ford.

"I Find No National Malaise"

Today Jimmy Carter is recognized as a good man of high moral character but regarded less highly as a president. By the middle of 1979, the beleaguered American economy was suffering from lagging growth, skyrocketing prices, and an energy crisis. Abroad, terrorists in Tehran, Iran held fifty-five Americans hostage for more than a year. Since 1974, the Soviet Union had brought nine countries into its ideological orbit: South Vietnam, Cambodia, Laos, South Yemen, Angola, Ethiopia, Mozambique, Grenada, and Nicaragua. In July 1979 a besieged President Carter appeared on national television to deliver what came to be known as his "malaise" speech. He told Americans that they were suffering from a "crisis of confidence...that strikes at the very heart and soul and spirit of our national will." By Christmas week the Soviets had boldly marched into Afghanistan with more than 100,000 troops.

From his retreat in the Santa Ynez Mountains, Reagan saw that he was needed again. "I find no national malaise," he said. "I find nothing wrong with the American people." What he did see was a weakening of the national defenses. He was widely criticized for opposing the unratified Strategic Arms Limitation Treaty (SALT II) signed by Carter and Soviet Premier Leonid

After mounting a strong challenge in the primaries, Reagan failed to win the nomination at the 1976 Republican convention. But once again, his call for unity rallied the party. "Nancy and I, we aren't going to go back and sit in our rocking chairs and say that's all for us," he assured his supporters. "Don't get cynical, because look at yourselves and what you were willing to do, and recognize that there are millions and millions of Americans out there that want what you want, that want it to be as we do, who want it to be a shining city on a hill. . . . You just stay in there. The cause is there and the cause will prevail because it's right."

Brezhnev in 1979. After being briefed by both the Carter administration and his own defense experts, Reagan concluded that SALT II was "fatally flawed" because it allowed the superpowers to increase their nuclear arsenals rather than reduce them. He said as much and was criticized even more.

That was also the year he visited the headquarters of the North American Aerospace Defense Command deep in the Rocky Mountains, where sophisticated equipment monitors U.S.

missiles and hostile ones that might be headed our way. Reagan was shocked to learn that the United States had no real defense against a missile attack beyond a fifteen-minute warning. We could accept an attack and do nothing, or we could retaliate and start a global nuclear war; there was no other alternative. This was known as MAD—Mutual Assured Destruction—and Reagan did not like it at all. He wanted a third choice: protection from nuclear attack.

Reagan campaigning in 1980.

Reagan had met with Margaret Thatcher in London in 1975 and again in 1978. She was not yet the British prime minister, merely a conservative leader. She and Reagan discussed the threat of Soviet missiles. Thatcher reminded him that while the United States was concerned about the prospect of intercontinental missiles, the Soviets already had powerful missiles aimed at every capital in western Europe. "We must stand together," she told him. It was the beginning of a remarkable alliance.

In the summer of 1980, President Carter fought a bitter battle for his own party's nomination in the state primaries, beating back a strong challenge from Senator Edward M. Kennedy. In the Republican primaries, candidate Ronald Reagan joined a crowded field of distinguished Republicans all vying for the presidential

nomination. They included George Bush, Senator Robert Dole, Congressman John Anderson, Congressman Philip Crane, Senator Howard Baker, and Governor John Connelly, and they represented a broad spectrum of beliefs. Reagan stuck to the message he had been putting forth since his first campaign for governor: balance the budget, reduce taxes, and restore the nation's defenses.

"I'm Paying for This Microphone, Mr. Green"

One of the most vivid moments of the 1980 Republican primaries came that winter in New Hampshire when Reagan insisted that a debate sponsored by a local newspaper, the *Nashua Telegraph*, had to include not just himself and frontrunner George Bush, as the newspaper had originally planned, but the other five candidates as well. The paper withdrew its financial support at the last minute when Robert Dole, one of the candidates who had not been invited, complained to the Federal Elections Commission that the newspaper's support of the debate constituted an illegal contribution to the Bush and Reagan campaigns. Reagan's people offered to split the costs of the broadcast with the Bush camp. When they declined, Reagan assumed all the costs. Although the newspaper was no longer underwriting the debate, both sides agreed that they would continue to manage it.

As Nancy Reagan recalls in her autobiography, *My Turn*, "The other Republican candidates were angry about being excluded, and Ronnie thought they had a good case. But the executives of the newspaper, which seemed to be supporting George Bush, still preferred a two-man debate. So did the Bush camp."

Minutes before the debate, Reagan and the other candidates were still trying to work out a compromise with the Bush team,

Late in the 1980 campaign, Reagan's confidence and exuberance were infectious and inspiring.

which would not budge. Word arrived that Bush was on stage, and if Reagan did not join him in five minutes, the debate would be canceled and Bush would be declared the winner. At that point, Nancy Reagan suggested that they all just go out together. And they did.

Reagan strolled onto the stage accompanied by Dole, Baker, Anderson, and Crane (Connelly was campaigning in South Car-olina), and the crowd of 2,500 went wild. The *Telegraph* editor who was moderating the event banged his gavel and said, "Mr. Reagan is out of order. Turn his microphone off."

"I'm paying for this microphone, Mr. Green," Reagan said mildly. In his excitement, he had mispronounced the moderator's name, which was John Breen. But his point was made, and that night he and his fellow Republicans were able to present a genuine

After a hard-fought primary campaign, Reagan chose his toughest rival, George Bush, as his running mate.

exchange of ideas. The experience revitalized Reagan and his campaign. On February 26 he took the New Hampshire primary with 51 percent of the vote. From there he swept the rest of the primaries, sailing into the Detroit convention that summer with more than enough votes to win the nomination.

A New Beginning

On July 17 Reagan accepted his party's nomination for president. In his acceptance speech, he rejected the idea that the United States had had its day and that our nation had passed its zenith. "The American people, the most generous on earth, who created the highest standard of living, are not going to accept the notion that we can only make a better world for others by moving backwards ourselves," he told the cheering crowd.

Reagan did surprise some supporters by choosing his former opponent, George Bush, as his running mate. Reagan was wise enough to recognize that Bush had exactly the qualities Reagan himself lacked: Bush was a veteran Washington insider, a former ambassador to the United Nations, a former chief of the U.S. Liaison Office in China, and a former director of the CIA. Reagan valued his experience and knew he could make an important contribution to a Reagan presidency.

Those who knew the real Reagan were not surprised at the manner in which he chose to conclude his acceptance speech. Looking out at the delegates, he said, "I'll confess I've been a little afraid to suggest what I'm going to suggest, what I'm going to say. I'm more afraid not to. Can we begin our crusade joined together in a moment of silent prayer?" The entire convention body rose immediately and the people bowed their heads. After a few seconds of meaningful silence, Reagan looked out at the great hall and said, "God bless America."

The Reagan campaign promised a new beginning, warned about the "window of vulnerability" created by Carter's cuts in military spending, and called for peace through strength. He rejected the Carter administration's MAD defense strategy. To him it limited the president to a choice between suicide or surrender. Carter was no match for Reagan's convictions. He tried to dismiss Reagan as ignorant for calling the 1980 economic downturn a depression. "That shows how little he knows," snapped Carter. "It's a recession." Reagan understood that semantics didn't mean much to the unemployed. "A recession is when your neighbor loses his job," he told one cheering crowd after another on the campaign trail. "A depression is when you lose yours. And recovery is when Jimmy Carter loses his!"

On October 28, he debated President Carter in Cleveland, Ohio. Carter was determined to paint Reagan as an extremist, but when he said that Reagan "began his political career campaigning against Medicare," Reagan responded, "There you go again." It

Thousands turned out to cheer Reagan and Bush on their final stop in the 1980 campaign, in Peoria, Illinois. Even former president Gerald Ford, Reagan's onetime rival, arrived to show support. Earlier in the campaign, Reagan had visited Ford carrying an Indian peace pipe, an artifact that Ford treasures to this day.

became the catchphrase for the last days of Reagan's campaign. Even more memorable was the question he put to the American public at the end of the debate: "Are you better off today than you were four years ago?"

On November 4, 1980, Ronald Wilson Reagan was elected the fortieth president of the United States by an electoral landslide. He won 43,899,248 votes to Carter's 35,481,435, which translated into 489 electoral votes for Reagan and 49 for Carter.

Chapter Five

THE
REAGAN
REVOLUTION

1981–1989

"They called it the Reagan Revolution.
Well, I'll accept that, but for me it always seemed more like the
great rediscovery, a rediscovery of our values and common sense."

—Ronald Reagan, Farewell Address to the nation, 1989

The new occupant of the White House was known to sharpen his own pencils and fetch his own coffee. He drafted his speeches on yellow legal pads, and he copied the finished product in his personal shorthand onto a handy pack of four- by six-inch index cards. Out of respect, he always made a point of wearing a jacket and tie when he was working in the Oval Office. He never passed White House doormen, any groundskeepers, or other staff without acknowledging them. He also liked to snack on jelly-beans and kept a full jar on his desk for visitors. He liked people and they liked him. But the Reagan presidency, quickly dubbed the Reagan Revolution, was about more than style.

Even before his inauguration on January 20, 1981, President-elect Ronald Reagan was at work forming his cabinet and the policies of his new administration. His agenda was clear: cut taxes, trim domestic programs, and increase military spending. His economic plan was simple: private ownership, free markets, sound money, and lower taxes. This became known as Reaganomics. Reagan believed that only lower tax rates could spur economic productivity.

One of his greatest concerns was the spread of communism throughout the world. The arrogance of the Soviet Union had increased during his predecessor's four years in the White House,

ABOVE: Reagan was sworn in as President of the United States on January 20, 1981. Supreme Court Justice Warren Burger administers the oath of office as Nancy holds the Bible that had belonged to Nelle Reagan. Senator Mark Hatfield, Chairman of the Joint Congressional Committee on Inaugural Ceremonies, stands behind her. PAGE 86: Reagan and Mikhail Gorbachev listen to "The Star Spangled Banner" during a White House welcoming ceremony, on December 8, 1987.

and Reagan was determined to cut the Soviets down to size. He made this clear on January 29, at the first news conference of his presidency, when he answered a question from the ABC network's Sam Donaldson about the Soviets: "The only morality they recognize is what will further their cause, meaning they reserve unto themselves the right to commit any crime, to lie, to cheat." No one ever had to ask Reagan how he really felt.

"Please Tell Me You're All Republicans"

On March 30, 1981, President Reagan was shot and seriously wounded by a deranged young man outside the Washington Hilton. At first, Reagan did not even realize that he had been hit. He heard a noise that sounded like firecrackers as he came out of the hotel and headed for his limousine. The next thing he knew, one of his Secret Service agents, Jerry Parr, had seized him by the waist and was pushing him headfirst into the limousine. Reagan later recalled the experience in his second autobiography, *An American Life*: "I landed on my face atop the armrest across the back seat and Jerry jumped on top of me. When he landed, I felt a pain in my upper back that was unbelievable. It was the most excruciating pain that I had ever felt. 'Jerry,' I said, 'Get off. I think you've broken one of my ribs.'" The shot that hit Reagan had actually careened off the

ABOVE: Bodyguards rush to shield the president after shots rang out outside the Washington Hilton on March 30, 1981. BELOW: Immediately after the shooting, there was chaos on the street, but the president was already on his way to the emergency room.

side of the limo and hit him as he was diving into the car. It entered under his left arm, hit a rib, and lodged within an inch of his heart.

On the sidewalk, his popular press secretary, James Brady, lay gravely wounded. Also hit were Washington policeman Thomas K. Delahanty and Secret Service agent Timothy McCarthy. The president's limousine raced to George Washington Hospital as the seventy-year-old president coughed up blood, soaking through his own handkerchief and then Parr's. He was struggling to breathe and could barely stand by the time they reached the hospital, but

This series of photos shows how quickly the Secret Service reacted to the shooting, even before Reagan himself knew what had happened.

If courage is grace under pressure, Reagan demonstrated the quality in abundance. "Please tell me you're all Republicans," he said to the doctors who quickly prepared him for the operating room. One surgeon assured him, "Today, we're all Republicans, Mr. President."

Nancy Reagan rushed to the hospital immediately upon receiving the news that her husband had been shot. She arrived there not knowing if he was alive or dead and learned he was already in the operating room. After surgery, she kept a vigil at his bedside until, emerging from the anesthesia and seeing her worried, frightened face, he said, "Honey, I forgot to duck." Presidential biographer Lou Cannon described another incident later that night: With tubes still in his throat that prevented him from speaking to a visitor, Reagan signaled for his notepad. "All in all, I'd rather be in Philadelphia," he wrote. Reagan's heroic behavior in this crisis—with no index cards, no TelePrompTer, no speechwriter, no handlers—strengthened his support from all Americans.

"A Campaign for Democracy"

Reagan refused to let an assassin's bullet slow down the progress of his agenda. Time was even more precious now. He used his personal recovery time to think about ways to achieve some kind of peace with the Soviet Union without compromise. While still recovering from his wounds in the hospital, he worked on a handwritten letter to Premier Brezhnev. He reminded Brezhnev of their first meeting, when he had visited President Nixon at San Clemente in 1973, and noted to him that they were both responsible for the hopes and dreams of millions of people.

A side effect of his brush with death was that, on his doctors' orders, he began lifting weights and doing bench presses, adding

he insisted on walking in under his own power. Inside, near collapse, he was immediately strapped to a gurney. A nurse took his pulse as he slipped in and out of consciousness. As she held his hand, he sought to ease the concern in her face by joking, "Does Nancy know about us?" Moments later, Reagan was in an operating room, where he underwent surgery for removal of a bullet that had narrowly missed his aorta. "If five minutes had been lost, he would have died," said Dr. David Gens, one of Reagan's surgeons.

Ronald and Nancy Reagan look splendid in formal attire, in 1981.

two inches to his chest. Less than a month after the shooting, the seventy-year-old president addressed a joint session of Congress on behalf of his economic recovery plan. In July he made good on a campaign pledge and nominated the first female justice to the Supreme Court. After confirmation by the Senate, Sandra Day O'Connor was sworn in that September.

Early in June 1982, President Reagan's first official visit to western Europe coincided with several foreign policy crises. Israel had invaded its neighbor Lebanon. The United Nations Security Council was debating a resolution on sanctions against Britain over the Falklands War. Reagan was determined to persuade his European allies not to go through with their agreement to help construct a $100 billion Soviet pipeline that would bring natural gas from Siberia to western Europe and provide Moscow with badly needed hard currency.

On June 8, Reagan addressed the British Parliament at the Palace of Westminster, and he delivered one of his finest speeches. He announced "a campaign for democracy" and pledged that the United States would support those who were fighting against communism "wherever we find them." He cited Poland, where a Soviet puppet government had met Solidarity's calls for freedom by declaring martial law. "It is the Soviet Union that runs against the tide of human history by denying human freedom and human dignity to its citizens," he declared. The Kremlin stepped up its international propaganda campaign to portray Reagan as a dangerous man and themselves as peace-loving.

Star Wars vs. the Evil Empire

On March 8, 1983, Reagan warned about "the aggressive impulses of the evil empire" in a headline-making speech at the National

Reagan meets with Secretary of State George Shultz and various other cabinet members. "He wanted America to be strong in every way," Shultz recalled. "He managed to get the United States into a much stronger position than it had been."

Association of Evangelicals in Orlando, Florida. Communism, he said, was "another sad bizarre chapter in human history." He was putting the Soviets on notice that this president had no illusions about their intentions. Some in the press were offended and fearful, but Reagan understood communists from his years of battling them in the entertainment industry. Whatever their differences, they respected straight talk.

Two weeks later, on March 23, Reagan concluded a nationally televised speech on the defense budget with a surprise call to America's men and women in uniform, scientists and engineers, entrepreneurs and industrial leaders, and all American citizens to join him in taking a bold step forward in defense. With that he announced the Strategic Defense Initiative (SDI), a high-tech program of satellite-mounted lasers capable of blasting incoming Soviet intercontinental missiles out of the sky. Reagan pledged to support SDI research and development completely. The press and his detractors greeted the idea with scorn and derision, quickly dubbing this visionary plan "Star Wars."

The detractors did not bother Reagan, who knew that American scientists had handed him a powerful new bargaining chip. Typically, he saw the potential for peace in an instrument of war. Reagan was convinced that if such a system could be made, say, 80 or 90 percent effective, that was as good as 100 percent, for it would persuade the other side that it was hopeless—and self-defeating—to mount an attack at all. In announcing the United States' commitment to SDI, Reagan was signaling to the Soviet Union that Americans had the political will and the economic might to create a strategic defense and intended to do so. Reagan has always been convinced that this announcement marked the beginning of the end of the Soviet Union.

The rest of 1983 was tumultuous: In September the Soviets shot down a Korean Air Lines passenger plane that had strayed over Siberia, killing the 269 people aboard, including sixty-one American citizens. Reagan was outraged but knew his response had to be measured. He condemned the Soviets, calling the incident a "crime against humanity." Unabashed, the Soviets charged that the flight had been on a spy mission for the United States. This only strengthened Reagan's resolve to take a hard line with the Soviets, but he had to bide his time.

"The Saddest Day of My Presidency"

One of the worst moments of Reagan's first term came on October 23, 1983, when 242 U.S. Marines were killed in Beirut by a car bomb driven into their barracks by a Shiite Muslim on a suicide mission. Reagan was especially anguished by this because the marines had been peacekeeping forces sent to maintain order in the middle of Lebanon's civil war. Reagan later called it "the saddest day of my presidency, perhaps the saddest day of my life." He

had met many of these men and seen their letters to their families. He was their commander in chief. Recognizing a no-win situation and unwilling to shed more American blood to support it, he soon pulled out the rest of the troops.

Operation Fury

Four days after the Beirut debacle, however, Reagan launched the Grenada rescue, the first successful American effort to restore democracy to a communist country. Small in size, Grenada was strategically located for Cuba's communist regime to provide support to the Sandinista government in Nicaragua, thus creating another communist country, one very close to the United States. Reagan was alerted that the United States had only twenty-four hours to stem a planned Soviet invasion of Grenada. U.S. spy satellites had detected an airstrip on Grenada that was entirely too ambitious for civilian use on such a tiny island. In addition, one thousand American citizens were living on the Caribbean island,

Reagan talks with Vice President George Bush and Henry Kissinger in the Oval Office, on July 25, 1983. "Ronald Reagan's most important contributions to the nation were his decency, his sense of honor, and the deep feeling he conveyed to the entire world that America is the greatest country on the face of the earth," Bush said recently.

On November 9, 1985, the Reagans entertained the Prince and Princess of Wales in the West Sitting Hall of the White House.

most of them students at St. George's Medical College, and they were also at risk.

When the Organization of Eastern Caribbean States sought the help of the United States, Reagan took immediate action. On October 25, in Operation Fury, about two thousand American troops, along with units from six Caribbean states, stormed the island of Grenada and battled the Marxist troops and remarkably well-armed Cuban "construction workers" for three days until the Marxist regime was ousted.

Instead of celebrating this blow against Soviet influence in our hemisphere, Reagan's opponents in Congress were outraged. Senator Walter Mondale warned that the Grenada invasion "undermines our ability to effectively criticize what the Soviets have done in their brutal intervention in Afghanistan, in Poland and elsewhere." There were calls for Reagan to resign, and a group of congressmen submitted a resolution that called for the president to be impeached for violating international law. The United Nations voted to condemn the U.S. action. But a year later, after

Reagan greets Pope John Paul II in Miami, on September 10, 1987. Both men had survived near-fatal assassination attempts.

the U.S. forces had withdrawn and documents had been unearthed that revealed the Marxist regime's plans to make the island a base for Soviet bloc activities and confirmed the true nature of the Cuban "construction workers," Reagan came to the island to celebrate the first anniversary of the rescue. He was hailed as a liberator.

Grenada was a tiny island, but this rescue marked the first time since the Vietnam War that the United States had committed troops and emerged victorious. It was the first time in more than half a century that a communist takeover of an independent nation was reversed by military action. It was Reagan's first blow against the evil empire.

"4 More in '84"

By the end of 1983, the Reagan presidency was regarded as a success. It had seen the passage of a 25 percent tax cut and a $181 billion increase in defense spending. Reagan was determined to accomplish even more, and on January 29, 1984, he announced that he would seek a second term. In the November election he opposed the Democratic nominee, former vice president Walter Mondale, who was running with the first woman nominated for vice president, New York congresswoman Geraldine Ferraro.

Once again, Reagan's sense of humor helped him. As Reagan and Mondale prepared to debate, the president was asked by reporters whether age would be an issue. Reagan responded: "No! I will not allow Mr. Mondale's youth to become an issue in these debates or on the presidential campaign." Reagan's first televised debate with Mondale was disappointing, but he rallied for the second. At one point during rehearsals for the second debate, Nancy Reagan, wrapped in a trenchcoat, stepped in front of him and opened her coat flasher-style. On her sweater was a sign that read "4 More in '84." It was just the laugh he needed.

Reagan looks pensive on November 1, 1983, shortly after the successful invasion of Grenada.

In November the West German government narrowly voted to accept U.S. Pershing II missiles. The next day, the Soviets walked out of the Geneva arms talks, which had begun two years earlier to negotiate an Intermediate Nuclear Forces (INF) Treaty. Reagan was sure they would be back. He believed that "you don't get into a war by being too strong. You get into wars by being too weak."

The Great Communicator

Reagan was reelected with 59 percent of the popular vote. He carried every state in the Union except for Mondale's home state, Minnesota. He racked up a total of 526 electoral votes, the greatest number ever tallied by a presidential candidate. At seventy-three he became the oldest American to win a presidential election. He intended to use his second term to open a new relationship with the Soviet Union and defrost the Cold War.

During his reelection campaign in 1984, Reagan agreed to debate his Democratic challenger, former Vice President Walter Mondale. After a disappointing performance at the first debate, Reagan bounced back in the second.

By now, friends and foes alike were calling Ronald Reagan "the Great Communicator." Reagan insisted that it was not his style or even his words that earned him that title; it was his message. "I wasn't a great communicator," he said, "but I communicated great things. And they didn't spring full bloom from my brow, they came from the heart of a great nation—from our experience, our

Treasury Secretary Donald Regan and Senate Majority Leader Robert Dole (both far left), joined prominent Republican and Democratic congressmen including Chairman of the House Ways and Means Committee Dan Rostenkowski to witness President Reagan signing the Tax Reform Act of 1986. The new law cut taxes for millions of Americans and closed billions of dollars worth of special-interest tax loopholes.

wisdom and our belief in the principles that have guided us for two centuries." In his February 1985 State of the Union address, Reagan said, "We must not break faith with those who are risking their lives on every continent from Afghanistan to Nicaragua to defy the Soviet-supported aggression and secure rights that have been ours since birth... support for freedom fighters is self-defense." This was the essence of the Reagan Doctrine.

He went to work preparing for resumed arms talks with Soviet leader Konstantin Chernenko. But on March 10, the day the

American and Soviet arms negotiators arrived in Geneva, Chernenko died in Moscow. His successor, Mikhail Gorbachev, announced in July that he would meet with President Reagan at Geneva for the first United States–Soviet summit in seven years. In November, both sides gathered at a lakeside chateau in Geneva. On the afternoon of the first day, Reagan suggested that he and Gorbachev take a break from the formal session. They walked down a path to a small boathouse. Alone together except for their interpreters, the two men exchanged small talk about children. He

The Reagans pose with India's young prime minister Rajiv Gandhi and his wife Sonia at a state dinner in June 1985. Gandhi's mother, Prime Minister Indira Gandhi, had been assassinated in 1984, and he himself would be cut down in 1991, two years after resigning from office.

Reagan's friendship with Ferdinand Marcos dated back to 1969, when then President Richard M. Nixon sent him on a mission to the strategically important Philippines. But when Philippine government corruption proved intolerable, Reagan prevailed on Marcos to step down and accept exile in Hawaii.

later described the encounter to Pete Wilson, a former governor of California. According to Wilson, Reagan looked directly into Gorbachev's eyes and in a wistful tone said, "I do hope for the sake of our children that we can find some way to avert this terrible, escalating arms race." As Reagan paused, Gorbachev—thinking the president had completed his thought—smiled slyly, unable to mask a sudden look of triumph in his eyes. After several seconds, Gorbachev opened his mouth to respond to the President, but before he could, Reagan continued, "Because if we can't, America will not lose it, I assure you." The rest of their private chat lasted more than an hour, and the two leaders emerged with an agreement for two future superpower summits, one in Washington and one in Moscow.

Once again, Reagan's sense of humor did not fail him. After his momentous meeting with Gorbachev, he returned to his own villa, where aides were waiting eagerly for a report. Longtime aide

Kenneth Adelman recalled in *Recollections of Reagan*: "He asked us to wait in the dining room while he went to the rest room. When he joined us, he had a big grin on his face. We began to realize that while he was in the rest room, he had taken his left arm out of his jacket sleeve, so now the sleeve hung limply. He looked down, grabbed the sleeve, and said, 'Where's my arm? It was here this morning before I met Gorbachev.'" Still, he was impressed with Gorbachev and told his aides that this was "a new kind of Soviet leader." At the end of the summit, Reagan and Gorbachev shook hands and signed a pledge to reduce their nuclear arsenals.

Reagan's strong stance in negotiating with the Soviet Union eventually led him and Mikhail Gorbachev—the two most powerful men in the world—to sign the Intermediate-range Nuclear Force (INF) treaty in the East Room of the White House, December 8, 1987.

"Out of the Ashes — Hope"

Reagan's controversial visit to the Bitburg cemetery in April 1985 was scheduled with the best of intentions. German chancellor Helmut Kohl suggested that Reagan visit a German graveyard as part of the commemoration of the fortieth anniversary of the end of World War II. It was meant to show how the two countries had overcome their differences and become allies. But shortly after the visit was announced, it was revealed that of the two thousand German soldiers buried at Bitburg, nearly fifty had been members of Hitler's SS. Controversy swirled around the visit, but Reagan refused to cancel, even when *The New York Times* said it threatened to become "the biggest fiasco of the Reagan presidency." He had given his word to Kohl, a loyal American ally.

However, out of respect to victims of the Holocaust, he stopped first at the Bergen-Belsen concentration camp. Typically, his general remarks there were optimistic: "Here, death ruled. But we have learned something as well. Because of what happened, we found that death cannot rule forever.... We are here because humanity refuses to accept that freedom, or the spirit of man, can ever be extinguished.... Out of the ashes—hope; and from all the pain—promise."

A conference table confrontation, with Secretary of State George Shultz at Reagan's left. "He preferred to get something done rather than to get credit for it," said Shultz. "That's the way he always behaved."

Reagan to Gorbachev: "Nyet"

Although only two more superpower summits were scheduled, Mikhail Gorbachev suddenly asked for an interim business meeting. Thus it was that on October 11, 1985, Reagan and Gorbachev met for the second time in the tiny capital city of Reykjavik, Iceland, for preliminary discussions on arms control. They came close to agreeing on massive reductions of their nuclear arsenals. Then Gorbachev surprised Reagan by offering to eliminate all the medium-range missiles in Europe and to cut the Soviet strategic arsenal by 50 percent. In exchange, the United States would have to agree to restrict SDI research, testing, and development.

> *"Reagan pushed me one step more and then one step more till we got to the precipice, and then he wanted one step more."*
>
> —Mikhail Gorbachev

Reagan's favorite Russian phrase had become "Doveryai, no proveryai" ("Trust, but verify"), but in this case, his response was a flat "Nyet." As Reagan stood up and donned his coat, Gorbachev pleaded: "Can't we do something about this?" "No," Reagan answered. "It's too late." The meeting was over.

Reagan knew that Gorbachev, with his deteriorating, fragile Soviet economy, could never match the costs of the U.S. SDI program. Many believe that it was SDI more than any other factor that broke the will of the Soviets. They realized they could no longer afford to compete militarily with the United States. Their economy could no longer sustain the burden.

Reagan did more than walk away from Gorbachev at Reykjavik. He next persuaded the West German government to station cruise missiles in West Germany, effectively neutralizing another major category of Soviet missiles that threatened western Europe.

Reagan knocks his head while responding to a reporter's question during a news conference at the White House on March 19, 1987. The beleaguered president fielded questions about the Iran-Contra episode; he would never believe that it had been an arms for hostages deal.

Iran-Contra

A month after the meeting at Reykjavik, Reagan faced the most serious crisis of his presidency when the Iran-Contra scandal broke. The first revelation was that high government officials had secretly sold arms to Iran in exchange for the release of American hostages held by Shiite Muslim terrorists in Lebanon. This violated Reagan's pledges to the American people that he would never make deals with terrorist governments. Worse news came when it

RONALD REAGAN, NEGOTIATOR

In 1990, Reagan gave a speech in Fulton, Missouri, at Westminster College Cold War Memorial, the spot where Winston Churchill had given the famous talk in which he said, "From Stetten in the Baltic to Trieste in the Adriatic, an iron curtain has descended across the Continent," in March 1946. Reagan discussed how the Cold War between the United States and the Soviet Union had come to an end and how democracy was restored all over:

For years it had been suggested by some opinion-makers that all would be well in the world if only the United States lowered its profile. Some of them would not only have us lower our profile—they would also lower our flag. I disagreed. I thought that the 1980s were a time to stop apologizing for America's legitimate national interests, and start asserting them.

I was by no means alone. Principled leaders like Helmut Kohl and Margaret Thatcher reinforced our message that the West would not be blackmailed and that the only rational course was to return to the bargaining table in Geneva and work out real and lasting arms reductions fair to both sides.

A new Soviet leader appeared on the scene, untainted by the past, unwilling to be shackled by crumbling orthodoxies. With the rise of Mikhail Gorbachev came the end of numbing oppression. Glasnost introduced openness to the world's most closed society. Perestroika held out the promise of a better life, achieved through democratic institutions and a market economy. And real arms control came to pass, as an entire class of weapons was eliminated for the first time in the atomic age.

Within months the Soviet Empire began to melt like a snowbank in May.

Back in June 1987, I stood in the free city of West Berlin and asked Mr. Gorbachev to tear down the wall.

Was he listening? Whether he was or not, neither he nor the rulers of Eastern Europe could ignore the much louder chants of demonstrators in the streets of Leipzig and Dresden and dozens of other German cities. In the churches and the schools, in the factories and on the farms, a once silent people found their voice and with it a battering ram to knock down walls, real and imagined. Because of them, the political map of Europe has been rewritten.

Reagan and Gorbachev shared a laugh in front of a fireplace on November 19, 1985, at their historic first meeting in Geneva. Reagan sensed immediately that Gorbachev was "new kind of Soviet leader."

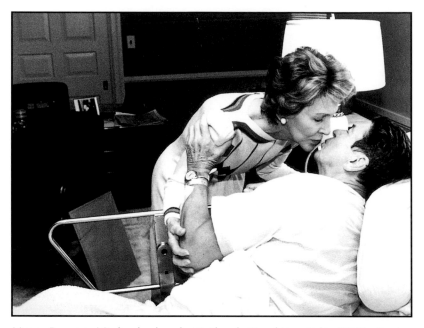

Nancy Reagan visits her husband at Bethesda Naval Hospital in 1987, after he underwent surgery. "I didn't have cancer," he insisted. "I had something inside of me that had cancer in it, and it was removed."

was revealed that the profits from these arms sales were used to support the anti-Sandinista rebels known as Contras in Nicaragua. This violated a congressional ban on aid to the Contras.

On March 19, 1987, Reagan held a nationally televised press conference in the East Room of the White House. Fielding a barrage of questions from an often hostile press, he insisted that he had never approved trading arms for hostages; it had been done

"Reagan's style wasn't to take every concession as final, settling in for what had been achieved. Always it was only the first step."

—Jeanne Kirkpatrick, United States ambassador to the United Nations, 1981–1985

without his knowledge. His sincerity reclaimed his reputation. Three separate investigations, including one by independent prosecutor Lawrence Walsh, concluded that there was no evidence that Reagan directed or even knew about the funds to the Contras. It was the lowest point in his presidency, but his greatest foreign policy triumphs still lay ahead.

Facing the Enemy

In January Reagan was operated on for prostate cancer. On October 17, Nancy was operated on for breast cancer. Together, the Reagans made a decision to go public with the fact that good medical supervision, early detection, and prompt treatment were the keys to victory over the disease. "People need to know that cancer isn't something to run and hide from," he would later say, in a 1990 address to the American Cancer Society. "Cancer is a fact that must be faced and dealt with."

On June 12, 1987, Reagan stood in the free city of West Berlin. In an address before the Brandenburg Gate and the Berlin Wall, he called for Gorbachev to tear down the divider. Defying his advisors, Reagan stood at the Brandenburg Gate and demanded, "Mr. Gorbachev, open up this gate! Mr. Gorbachev, tear down this wall!" He boldly predicted, "This wall will fall." And it did—just over two years later.

On December 8, Reagan and Gorbachev met in Washington, D.C., at a superpower summit, where they signed an INF Treaty to eliminate all Pershing II and SS-20 intermediate-range missiles in Europe. This was a sincere major first step toward serious disarmament.

Reagan arrived in Moscow for the fourth and final summit of his presidency in the spring of 1988. The previous month, the

"Mr. Gorbachev, open up this gate! Mr. Gorbachev, tear down this wall!" Reagan demanded in June 1987, as he stood outside the Brandenburg Gate at the Berlin Wall. He was flanked by West German Parliament President Philip Jenninger (left) and West German Chancellor Helmut Kohl (right).

Soviets had agreed to withdraw from Afghanistan. Gorbachev was in the process of opening the Soviet system with his policies of perestroika, or restructuring, and glasnost. In a radical, daring speech, Reagan addressed the students at Moscow State University and invited Soviet dissidents to speak their minds at the U.S. embassy.

ABOVE: Reagan met with Secretary of State George Shultz in the Oval Office on February 19, 1988, to discuss Schultz's pre-summit meetings with Kremlin leadership. Lt. Gen. Colin Powell, Chairman of Joint Chiefs of Staff, and White House Chief of Staff Howard Baker also attended. OPPOSITE: "It was hard to say good-bye," said Reagan as he and the First Lady left Washington on January 20, 1989. "It's been a time of tears for a great many people and certainly for us. But returning to California means a return to a life we love very much."

Sweet Sorrow

"People ask how I feel about leaving. And the fact is, parting is such sweet sorrow."

—Reagan's Farewell Address to the nation, 1989

Although Reagan remained hugely popular, the Twenty-second Amendment limited the presidency to two terms. As Reagan's presidency drew to a close, as many as fourteen distinguished Republicans vied for the chance to succeed him. They ranged from Senator Robert Dole to the Reverend Pat Robertson and Congressman Jack Kemp. Vice President George Bush fought for the job in statewide primaries and won the nomination and Reagan's endorsement. In the November 1988 election, Bush and his running mate, Senator Dan Quayle, faced Democratic nominee Michael Dukakis, the liberal governor from Massachusetts, and veteran Texas Senator Lloyd Bentsen. Dukakis was a member of the American Civil Liberties Union and opposed the reciting of the Pledge of Allegiance in public schools, among other things. The election amounted to a referendum on the Reagan presidency, and the election of George Bush as forty-first president of the United States was the voters' final endorsement of the Great Communicator.

Chapter Six

THE REAGAN LEGACY

1989–

"It's been my honor to be your president."

—Ronald Reagan, Farewell Address to the nation, 1989

It was time for the citizen-politician to return to private life. He left the White House with the highest popularity rating of any president in the past forty years. Ronald Reagan delivered his farewell address to the nation on January 11, 1989. He spoke with a mixture of sadness and optimism. He was sad to be leaving the White House, his home for eight years, but he was pleased that George Bush, his vice president of two terms, had been elected to succeed him by a resounding 53 percent, becoming the first sitting vice president to ascend to the presidency since Martin Van Buren in 1837.

He was proud of the legacy he was leaving behind. He had ended the Cold War, vanquished the mighty Soviet empire, and presided over one of the greatest economic expansions in history. Reagan was most proud of America's economic recovery, and he credited the American people for creating nineteen million new jobs and tens of thousands of new businesses during his eight years in office. He was just as proud of restoring the nation's morale. The United States was once again respected as the acknowledged leader of the free world.

Reagan wanted to see a new closeness with the Soviet Union, but he still believed that the United States must "trust, but verify." He called for an "informed patriotism," and he warned that America had to better convey that "America is freedom—freedom of speech, freedom of religion, freedom of enterprise. And freedom is precious and rare. It's fragile; it needs protection."

Throughout his years in government, Reagan often liked to compare the United States to "a shining city on a hill." He explained that to him, this place "was a tall, proud city built on rock stronger than oceans, windswept, God-blessed, and teeming with people of all kinds living in harmony and peace; a city with free ports that hummed with commerce and creativity." After two hundred years, that city was still a beacon for all who yearned for freedom.

Above: Reagan in his office at Century City, February 5, 1990. By 1994, Alzheimer's disease had begun to take its toll and he officially retreated from public appearances. Page 108: "President Reagan's message was a simple one," said his former Chairman of the Joint Chiefs of Staff, General Colin Powell. "It was sometimes seen as naïve, simplistic, and lacking in sophistication. It had the sole redeeming virtue of being right. And the world is a better place for his having been right."

A Birthday Wish

On January 29, after George Bush had been sworn in as the new president, an air force helicopter carrying Mr. and Mrs. Reagan lifted off from the eastern lawn of the White House. As the former president and his first lady left Washington, America was at peace, her defenses were strong, and she stood proud in the eyes of the world.

The decade to come would bring the fall of the Berlin Wall, the reunification of Germany, the collapse of the Soviet Union, the student uprising in Tiananmen Square, and the triumph of free elections from Chile to Czechoslovakia. None of these historic events would have happened without Ronald Reagan's presidency.

"I guess you and I have run against each other at least once," Reagan joked as he gathered with President Bush and former presidents Carter, Ford, and Nixon (left to right), before the dedication ceremonies for the Ronald Reagan Presidential Library in Simi Valley, California, on November 4, 1991.

Reagan acknowledged one disappointment: he had not been able to balance the federal budget. He announced that in the years to come he intended to dedicate himself to achieving that goal. He would also work to give the president a line-item veto. Reagan was convinced that this was the only way a president could enforce a balanced budget. Reagan was especially annoyed when opponents blamed his tax cuts for the federal deficit. The truth was that since he had reduced the tax rates in 1981, federal revenues had increased by $375 billion. But congressional spending had grown even faster, to $450 billion. "We don't have a budget deficit because we, our people, aren't taxed enough," he said frequently. "We have a deficit because the Congress spends too much."

The same day that Reagan turned the powers of the presidency to George Bush, he returned to California to his and Nancy's new home on St. Cloud Road in Bel Air. The ranch house was a far cry from the grandeur of the White House, but it was also a long way from the modest second-floor apartment in Tampico where he was born. Although the press often identified the Reagans as

Reagan and Gorbachev meet after their tenure as heads of state at Rancho del Cielo, May 3, 1992. Privately, Gorbachev expressed surprise at the modest one-story adobe ranch house.

having a luxurious lifestyle, friends knew that they had always lived relatively modestly. The same furniture that filled their new house had been with them since their days in Pacific Palisades, long before Ronald or Nancy Reagan could have dreamed of the phenomenal journey that would take them to Sacramento and Wash-ington, to meetings with kings and prime ministers. The world had changed a great deal since those quiet days as a private citizen, and Reagan himself could take credit for many of the changes.

He was the oldest man ever elected president; he had survived an assassination attempt and two cancer surgeries; yet he remained vigorous and active in retirement. He gave speeches and published newspaper articles and a second autobiography. On his trips to Germany, Poland, and Russia in those years he was greeted as a hero. His beloved country continued to honor him in the years to come. In the fall of 1991, President Bush and the three other surviving former presidents—Nixon, Ford, and Carter—joined Reagan for the dedication of the Ronald Reagan Presidential Library and Center for Public Affairs in Simi Valley, California.

The following February, Reagan celebrated his eighty-first birthday at a black-tie gala in Beverly Hills to raise money for the library. His longtime friend, former British prime minister Margaret Thatcher, was the featured speaker. That night, the former commander in chief told the more than nine hundred well-wishers that he wanted to "make a special birthday wish. My wish is that God will watch over each and every one of our men and women who are bravely serving in the Persian Gulf and their families wherever they may be. And they may know that we as a nation stand firmly behind them."

The Journey into the Sunset of His Life

Sadly, Reagan's active retirement did not continue much longer. In February 1994, he gave his last public speech at a Washington, D.C., celebration honoring his eighty-third birthday. The previous summer, during his annual physical checkup at the Mayo Clinic in Rochester, Minnesota, he had been diagnosed with Alzheimer's disease, and the illness had begun to take its toll. He and Nancy talked about whether to keep this a private matter. But they recalled how going public with their experiences with cancer had encouraged others to seek early treatment and save lives. On November 5, he announced his illness in a gallant handwritten letter:

The former president greets the former prime minister, Margaret Thatcher, at the Republican National Committee dinner, in 1994. "Ronald Reagan won the Cold War single-handedly, without firing a shot," said Mrs. Thatcher.

TRIBUTE FROM A FELLOW LEADER

Prime Minister of Great Britain Margaret Thatcher and Ronald Reagan shared many of the same philosophies in leading their nations: principled dedications to democracy and to laissez-faire economics. At Reagan's 1994 birthday gala, Margaret Thatcher saluted the fortieth President of the United States:

Sir, you strode into our midst at a time when America needed you most.... In a time of average men, you stood taller than anyone else.

With a toughness unseen for a long time, you stood face-to-face with the evil empire. And, with an unexpected diplomacy which confused your foes—and even some of your friends—you reached out to that empire, perhaps no longer evil, but still formidable. You met its leaders on their turf, but on your terms.

In a time of politicians, you proved yourself a statesman. ... It was not only that you were the Great Communicator—and you were the greatest—but that you had a message to communicate. ... Not since Lincoln, or Winston Churchill in Britain, has there been a President who has so understood the power of words to uplift and to inspire.

Reagan, at peace at his beloved ranch.

My fellow Americans,

I have recently been told that I am one of the millions of Americans who will be afflicted with Alzheimer's disease.

Upon learning this news, Nancy and I had to decide whether as private citizens we would keep this a private matter or whether we would make this news known in a public way.

In the past Nancy suffered from breast cancer and I had my cancer surgeries. We found through our open disclosures we were able to raise public awareness. We were happy that as a result many more people underwent testing.

They were treated in early stages and able to return to normal, healthy lives.

So now, we feel it is important to share it with you. In opening our hearts, we hope this might promote greater awareness of this condition. Perhaps it will encourage a clearer understanding of the individuals and families who are affected by it.

At the moment, I feel just fine. I intend to live the remainder of the years God gives me on this earth doing the things I have always done. I will continue to share life's journey with my beloved Nancy and my family. I plan to enjoy the great outdoors and stay in touch with my friends and supporters.

Unfortunately, as Alzheimer's disease progresses, the family often bears a heavy burden. I only wish there was some way I could spare Nancy from this painful experience. When the time comes I am confident that with your help she will face it with faith and courage.

In closing let me thank you, the American people, for giving me the great honor of allowing me to serve as your president. When the Lord calls me home, whenever that may be, I will leave the greatest love for this country of ours and eternal optimism for its future.

I now begin the journey that will lead me into the sunset of my life. I know that for America there will always be a bright dawn ahead.

Thank you, my friends. May God always bless you.

Reagan's announcement was greeted with praise for his characteristic candor and compassion for him and Nancy in this very difficult time.

"I salute President Reagan for his courage and sharing this private matter with the American people," said former president George Bush when he heard the news. President Clinton interrupted a political rally in Oakland, California. "A few minutes ago, President Reagan announced he was suffering from Alzheimer's

Reagan speaks at the dedication of the Ronald Reagan Presidential Library and Center for Public Affairs in 1991.

place was as grand as he'd expected," said Marc Short, the executive director of the YAF who, with his wife, Kristen, oversees the plans for the ranch. "You see how simple a man the president was," Short told interviewers in May 1998. "He really came out here to get away from Washington and didn't need a palace."

In his first inaugural address in 1981, Ronald Reagan asked his fellow Americans to "dream heroic dreams." The will to believe those dreams and to make them come true is still the heart and soul of the Reagan legacy.

disease," Clinton said. "And when he said it, it touched my heart in a particular way." He asked the crowd of more than four thousand Democrats to join him in wishing Reagan well.

There will be no more retreats to Rancho del Cielo, the rustic mountain hideaway high above Santa Barbara that Reagan had christened the "heavenly ranch." He made his last visit there in 1995, and two years later the Reagan family sold the property to the Young America's Foundation (YAF), a nonprofit group that plans to use it to educate college students about the Reagan legacy. Filled with photographs and memorabilia, it is said to look very much as it did during the twenty years Reagan spent there. From the dining room there is a view of Lake Lucky, which is not much more than a pond, where the Reagans kept their canoe called the True Love. Nearby is a round wooden picnic table where he signed Reaganomics into law in 1981. Gorbachev spent a day with the Reagans at the ranch in 1992. Although Reagan gave him a cowboy hat, he came away disappointed. "He didn't think the

In his last convention appearance, Ronald Reagan spoke at the Republican National Convention in Houston, in August 1992, calling for unity behind embattled President George Bush.

Bibliography

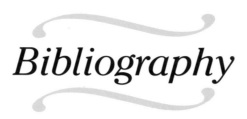

Colacello, Robert. "Ron and Nancy Part I." *Vanity Fair*, August 1998.

—————. "Ron and Nancy Part II: The White House Years and Beyond." *Vanity Fair*, September 1998.

Hannaford, Peter, ed. *Recollections of Reagan: A Portrait of Ronald Reagan*. New York: Morrow, 1997.

Reagan, Nancy, with William Novak. *My Turn: The Memoirs of Nancy Reagan*. New York: Random House, 1989.

Reagan, Ronald. *An American Life*. New York: Simon & Schuster, 1990.

Reagan, Ronald, with Richard G. Hubler. *Where's the Rest of Me?* New York: Duell, Sloan and Pearce, 1965.

Index

A

Accomplishments, 110–111
Albert, Eddie, 33, *51*
Alcohol, influence on, 11–13, 20
Alzheimer's Disease, 113–114
America, optimism about, 80, 84, 87
Americanness of Reagan, 10, 26, *35*
An American Life (autobiography), 88
An Angel from Texas (1940 film), 35
Appearance, charm of, *10, 21, 26, 35*
Army career, 20, 44–47, *44, 46, 47, 48*
Assassination attempt, 88–90, *89, 90*
Autobiographies, 40, 49, 88

B

The Bad Man (1941 film), *38*
Baker, Howard, *106*
Bancroft, Bass, 32
Bedtime for Bonzo (1951 film), 38
Berlin Wall, 65, 103, 104, 110
Bitberg cemetery, visit to, 100–101
Bogart, Humphrey, 31, 32, *45*
Brady, James, 89
Brewer, Roy M., *64*
Brezhnev, Leonid, 80–81, 90
Brother Rat (1938 film), *30, 31,* 33
Brother Rat and a Baby (1940 film), 35
Brown, Edmund G. "Pat," *54,* 71–72
Bryan, Jane, 35
Buckley, William F., *69*
Budget, balancing of, 111
Burger, Warren, *88*
Bush, George, 82, 84, *84, 85, 95,* 106, 110, *111,* 112, 114,

C

Cabinet, *92*
California
    governorship of, *68,* 69, 71–77, *72, 73*
    love of, 27–29, 69–71
Callahan, Mush, 32
Carter, Jimmy, 80, 82, *111,* 113
Casablanca (1942 film), *45*
Charles, Prince of Wales, *94*
Childhood, *8,* 11–15, *11*
Children, *34,* 38, 49–51, 62, 75
China, restored relations with, 77
Choy, Wilbur W. Y., *73*
Christianity, influence of, 11, 12, 13, 15, 20
Churchill, Winston, 38
Cleaver, Ben, 15
Cleaver, Margaret, 14, 15, 20
Clinton, Bill, 114–115
Code of the Secret Service (1939 film), 32
College years, 15–17, *15–17,* 20
Communicator, reputation as, 96–99
Communists, experiences with, 17, 32, 48, 50–55
The Conservatives (TV show), 69
The Cowboy from Brooklyn (1938 film), 35

D

Dancing, love of, 20
Daniels, Bebe, 41
Dark Victory (1939 film), *29,* 32
Dart, Justin, 35
Davis, Bette, *29,* 32,
Davis, Loyal, 58
Davis, Nancy. *See* Reagan, Nancy
Day, Doris, *51,* 58
Death Valley Days (TV show), 65
de Havilland, Olivia, 36
Desperate Journey (1942 film), 32, *40,* 44

Diana, Princess of Wales, *94*
Dickinson, Angie, 65, *65*
Dixon, Illinois, 12, 31, 41
Dole, Robert, 80, *98*
"Dutch" (nickname), origin of, 11

E

Eureka College, 15–17, 20, 50

F

Farewell address, 109, 110
Flynn, Errol, 36, *40,* 58
Fonda, Henry, *52*
Ford, Gerald, 78, *85,* 111, 113
Fulks, Sara Jane. *See* Wyman, Jane

G

Gandhi, Rajiv, *99*
General Electric, 62–63, 65, 68, *79*
The Gipper, 35–37
The Girl from Jones Beach (1949 film), 55, 57
Goldwater, Barry, 65, 68–70, *69,* 79
Gorbachev, Mikhail, *86,* 98–99, *100,* 101, 103, *103, 112* 115,
Government, attitude toward, 47, 50, 52, 67, 70, 71, 73–75, 77
Great Depression, impact of, 17–18, 50
Grenada, invasion of, 95–96

H

The Hasty Heart (1949 film), 57
Hearing problems, 32, 46

Hellcats of the Navy (1957 film), *59*, 65,
Heston, Charlton, 65
High school years, 13–15, *14*
Hodges, Joy, 20, 24, 32
Hollywood
career in, 23, *24–25*, *25*–41, *29*, *40*, 51–63, *52*,
    54, 56, 71,
union violence in, 51–52
Hollywood Hotel (1937 film), 31
Home Front (Patti Reagan), 75
Horseback riding, 20, 27, 32–33, *41*
House Un-American Activities Committee
    (HUAC), testimony before, *42*, 43, 52–53,
    53
Humphrey, Hubert, 69, 77

I

Illness and injury, 51, 57
    assassination attempt, 88–90, *89*, *90*
    prostate cancer, 104–105, *104*
Inaugurations
    as Gov. of California, 72–73, *73*
    as President, 12, 88, *88* 115,
Intermediate-range Nuclear Force (INF)
    Treaty, signing of, *100* 104,
International Squadron (1941 film), 32, 38, 41
Iran-contra episode, 102–104, *102*

J

Jezebel (1938 film), 32
John Loves Mary (1949 film), 55
Johnny Belinda (1948 film), 51
John Paul II, Pope, *95*
Johnson, Lyndon, 68, 69, 71
Juke Girl (1942 film), 44

K

Kennedy, Edward M., 82
Kennedy, John F., 65
Kennedy, Robert F., 75
The Killers (1964 film), 65, *65*
Kings Row (1942 film), 38–41, *39*, 44,
Kissinger, Henry, 78, *95*
Knute Rockne—All American (1940 film), 32,
    35–37, *36*, *37*
Kohl, Helmut, 103, *105*

Krushchev, Nikita, 65

L

Lane, Priscilla, 38
Laurie, Piper, 61
Law and Order (1953 film), *54*
Lenin, Vladimir, 52
Leslie, Joan, *46*
Lifestyle, 111–112, 115
The Lost Weekend (1944 film), 49
Louis, Joe, 47
Louisa (1950), 60
Love is on the Air (1937 film), *24*, 27, *27*, 29–31,
    32
Luckett, Edie, 58
Lyon, Ben, 41

M

Marcos, Ferdinand, *99*
Marine barracks in Beirut, car-bombing of, 95
Marriages
    first, 34, *34. 55*, *See also* Wyman, Jane
    second, 61–62, *63*. *See also* Reagan, Nancy
Marshall, Brenda, 61
Massey, Raymond, 36
Mayo, Virginia, 55
McComb, Marshall F., *73*
McGovern, George S., 77–78
McKinzie, Ralph "Mac," 17, 37
MGM Studios, 38
Milland, Ray, 49
Million Dollar Baby (1941 film), 38
Mondale, Walter, 94, 96
Morris, Wayne, *51*
Murder in the Air (1940 film), 32
Murphy, George, 47, *49*, 58, 73,
Mutual Assured Destruction (MAD), 81, 84
My Turn (Nancy Reagan), 68, 82

N

Neal, Patricia, 55, 57
The Next Voice You Hear (1950), 58
Night Unto Night (1949 film), 51
Nine Lives Are Not Enough (1941 film), 38
Nixon, Richard, 65, 71, 77–78, *99*, *111*, 113

O

O'Brien, Pat, 31, 35, 36, *37*
O'Connor, Sandra Day, 92
Operation Fury, 95–96

P

Paramount Studios, 49
Parents, 11–14, *11.* 16, 20, 31, *See* also,
    Reagan, John Edward; Reagan, Nelle
    Clyde
    father figures for, 15, 17
Parker, Eleanor, 55
Parr, Jerry, 88
Parsons, Louella, 31, 34, *34*, 41
Pearl Harbor attack, 44
Personality, 10, 33–34, 63, 75, 77, 88
Political life, entry into, 65, 68–72
Political opinions, early, 18, 35, 52, 55, 61
Powell, Colin, *106*
Powell, Dick, 31, 35
Presidency
    first term, 88–96
    second term, 97–106
Presidential campaign, 1976, 78–80, *80*, *81*
Presidential campaign, 1980, 82–85, *82–85*
Presidential campaign, 1984, 96, *97*
Presidential library, 113, *115*
Prohibition, 12–13, 20

R

Race relations, 14–15, 17, 35
Radio career, 18–20, *19*, 24, 26
Ranch life, 57, 111–112, *112*, *114*, 115
Reagan, John Edward "Jack," 11, 12, 13, 36
Reagan, John Neil "Moon," 11, 13, *13*, 20, 35
Reagan, Maureen Elizabeth, *34*, 38
Reagan, Michael, 49
Reagan, Nancy, 58, *59*, 60–62, *63*, 65, 68, 74,
    76, *80*, *81*, 85, 88, *91*, 96, *99*, 104, *104*,
    113, *115*
Reagan, Nelle Clyde Wilson, 11, 12, *12*, 61, 65
Reagan, Patricia Ann, 62, 74, *75*
Reagan, Ronald Jr., *74*, 75
Reaganomics, 88
Rear Gunner (1942 film), 47
Recollections of Reagan (Adelman), 99
Regan, Donald, *98*